MAKING OUR WAY

Making Our Way

AMERICA AT THE TURN OF THE CENTURY
IN THE WORDS OF THE POOR AND POWERLESS

selected by
WILLIAM LOREN KATZ
and
JACQUELINE HUNT KATZ

ILLUSTRATED WITH PHOTOGRAPHS

The Dial Press
New York

CARNEGIE PUBLIC LIBRARY
ROBINSON, ILLINOIS

*The frontispiece shows
a collar starcher carrying her laundry.*

Copyright © 1975 by Ethrac Publications, Inc.
All rights reserved. No part of this book may be reproduced
in any form or by any means without the prior written permission
of the publisher, excepting brief quotes used in connection with
reviews written specifically for inclusion in a magazine or newspaper.
Printed in the United States of America · First Printing
Design by Atha Tehon

Library of Congress Cataloging in Publication Data
Main entry under title:

Making our way.

Bibliography: p. Contents: Sadie Frowne, a sweatshop girl at sixteen.
—Antanas Kaztaukis, from Lithuania to the Chicago stockyards.
—An Anonymous farmer's wife.—Rocco Corresca, bootblack. [etc.]
1. Poor—United States—Addresses, essays, lectures—Juvenile literature.
2. United States—Social conditions—1865–1918—Addresses, essays,
lectures—Juvenile literature. [1. Poor—Addresses, essays, lectures.
2. United States—Social conditions—1865–1918—Addresses, essays,
lectures]   I. Katz, William Loren.   II. Katz, Jacqueline Hunt.
HC110.P6M28   301.44′1   74-18601
ISBN 0-8037-5442-6

*To Margaret Wilkie Hunt
and all those who have spent their lives in toil*

Contents

Introduction · ix

Sadie Frowne
A Sweatshop Girl at Sixteen
§ 3 §

Antanas Kaztaukis
From Lithuania to the Chicago Stockyards
§ 14 §

An Anonymous Farmer's Wife
§ 33 §

Rocco Corresca
Bootblack
§ 48 §

An Anonymous Georgia Sharecropper
§ 61 §

An Anonymous Irish Cook
§ 76 §

Ah-nen-la-de-ni
A Mohawk Tribesman
§ *83* §

An Anonymous Coal Miner
§ *97* §

Nat Love
Cowboy
§ *106* §

Lee Chew
Chinese American
§ *113* §

An Anonymous Collar Starcher
§ *126* §

Elias Garza
Mexican American
§ *140* §

An Anonymous Policeman
§ *146* §

Mariner J. Kent
The Making of a Tramp
§ *155* §

Recommended Reading · 167
Bibliographical Note · 169

Photograph inserts appear
after pages 78 and 110

Introduction

When one thinks of America at the turn of the century, colorful images come to mind: an ornate parlor with flickering gaslights, happy riders in a horse-drawn buggy, a picnic on the pristine banks of the Hudson, ladies dancing at a ball in elaborate, tightly laced dresses. Life was like that—for some.

But for many others it was a time of agonizing stress. As the nineteenth century drew to a close, the nation was climbing out of its worst economic depression to that date. A third of the railroads fell into receivership, *15,000* business concerns and *600* banks closed. In sparsely set-

Introduction

tled Colorado *30,000* men had no jobs. Chicago had *200,000* unemployed. America was going through a wrenching upheaval that left few lives unchanged. In the years following the Civil War, manufacturing had become king. A rural nation of small farms, skilled artisans, and hand-produced goods was transformed into a modern industrial world power.

Millions left the farmlands to find factory jobs—the unemployed, dispossessed, and disheartened as well as the adventurous. They were joined in the cities by millions of European immigrants searching for work. By *1900* New York City alone had a population greater by far than the five largest American cities of *1860* combined. Its laborers crowded into dilapidated tenements close to the smell and noise of their work. Gotham Court apartments at *36* Cherry Street offered large families two-room flats—one room nine by fourteen, the other nine by six feet—without plumbing, heat, or sunlight. This was considered a spacious home for a family of five and a suitable one for eight people. Each night as Jacob Riis walked his reporter's beat, he marveled at the capacity of human beings to survive in the city: "The wonder is that they are not all corrupted, and speedily, by their surroundings."

Urban corruption was widespread and commonly blamed on newcomers from Europe who inhabited the slums, crowded the jails, and, in return for small favors, voted for candidates of the political machines. Reporter Lincoln Steffens investigated corruption in city after city and found that "the machine controls the whole process of voting, and practices fraud at every stage." Not for-

Introduction

eigners, he concluded, but business interests "by bribery, corruption or somehow" controlled political machines and city governments. In Philadelphia, "the most American of our cities," Steffens saw voting lists padded with names of "dead dogs, children, and non-existent persons."

In their jobs, the urban poor, including two million children and five million women, faced low pay, grindingly dull and sometimes painful labor, periodic wage cuts, the threat of unemployment, and economic depressions. Employers reduced wages, locked out workers, and refused to bargain with unions. To smash employee resistance, they hired spies and regiments of armed men. "I can hire one half the working class to kill the other half," boasted financier Jay Gould, who manipulated men as easily as gold and stock prices.

When their private efforts failed, companies knew they could count on government aid in fighting their workers. Unions and strikes were considered conspiracies in restraint of trade, so local police, state militia, court injunctions, federal marshals, and the U.S. infantry stood ready to smash employee organizations. "We hire the law by the year," claimed a railroad owner.

This left the average person little choice but to labor at the dictate of a boss. For as little as four or five cents an hour, most Americans worked twelve hours a day, six days a week. In poorly lit, unventilated, and unsafe mines and mills, children and adults struggled to meet the demands of untiring machines and greedy men. Some were old at thirty; many died of overwork.

Child-labor laws were as yet nonexistent. In a textile

Introduction

factory, a government investigator found one child "fifty inches high and weighing perhaps forty-eight pounds, who works from six at night until six in the morning, and is so tiny that she has to climb up on the spinning frame to reach the top row of spindles." The accident rate for adults was high but for children it was double.

Unsafe conditions led to many early deaths. In *1911* a fire swept the Triangle Shirt Waist Company in New York City. In eighteen minutes *146* young women lost their lives. Rose Schneiderman, who had organized these garment workers and seen them beaten and jailed for union activities the year before, spoke at their memorial: "Every week I must learn of the untimely death of one of my sister workers. Every year thousands of us are maimed."

While economic necessity forced poor women and girls to work, affluent husbands and fathers controlled the lives of *their* wives and daughters. Home and kitchen were their prison. To speak for equal rights or women's suffrage brought derision or ostracism to any woman. The speaker was considered a threat to family, home, and society.

If conditions such as those described above were hardly bearable for men, women, and children of the white majority, circumstances were often altogether unbearable for the nonwhites living and working in America.

The *1890*s opened with the massacre of *350* Sioux men, women, and children by the U.S. Seventh Cavalry at Wounded Knee, South Dakota. "We tried to run," said one of the fifty survivors, "but they shot us like we were buffalo." For their part in the slaughter, eighteen U.S.

Introduction

cavalrymen were awarded the Congressional Medal of Honor.

Government policy forced these proud Native Americans onto reservations, where missionaries undermined their culture, religion, leaders, and families. T. J. Morgan, Commissioner of Indian Affairs, said, "We ask them to recognize that we [whites] are the better race; that our God is the true God; that our civilization is the better; that our manners and customs are superior." Whites defrauded Native Americans of millions of acres of land. "The love of possession," said Sitting Bull of whites, "is a disease with them."

At the turn of the century, *90* percent of Black Americans lived in the South; most were landless and voteless. While slavery had been abolished in *1863* by the Emancipation Proclamation, the Southern sharecropping system continued to hold millions of Blacks in a new bondage. "We make jest enough to keep in debt," reported one. To provide cheap and obedient labor, the law rounded up Blacks for minor or nonexistent crimes and rented them out as convicts for pennies a day. "The court and the man you work for are always partners," recounted one victim. "One makes the fine and the other works you and holds you, and if you leave you are tracked with bloodhounds and brought back."

Between *1890* and *1910,* every Southern state wrote into its basic laws provisions for the disenfranchisement of its Black citizens and for their segregation in all public facilities and conveyances. In *1896* a federal stamp of approval was placed on segregation when the Supreme Court ruled that racial separation did not violate the

Introduction

Constitution. While in *1905* W. E. B. Du Bois and his Niagara movement said: "We will not be satisfied to take one jot or tittle less than our full manhood rights," the best advice Booker T. Washington, leading Black spokesman of the day, could offer his people was, "When your head is in the lion's mouth, use your hand to pet him." Northern and Southern Blacks found their citizenship a mockery, their manhood a farce, their demands for justice unheard. They were portrayed degradingly in magazines, newspapers, popular songs, cartoons, nursery rhymes, and jokes. In *1900* a St. Louis Bible society published a book, *The Negro a Beast,* that sought to prove that Blacks lacked a soul. When addressing a group of Black college graduates, President William Howard Taft said, "Your race is adapted to be a race of farmers, first, last, and for all time."

Blacks were slain with impunity by lynch mobs, sometimes led by law-enforcement officers and encouraged by clergymen, senators, and governors. "If it is necessary, every Negro in the state will be lynched," shouted Governor James Vardman of Mississippi. "It will be done to maintain white supremacy." Between *1889* and *1901* more than two thousand Black men, women, and children died at the hands of mobs.

Meanwhile, in the Southwest, Mexican Americans (Chicanos) were treated much like Native Americans and Blacks, that is, as citizens without rights or dignity. Many had been forced to accept American government after the Mexican War of *1848* brought under U.S. control territory that had previously been Mexico's; now

Introduction

they found themselves left without equal protection under the white man's law.

The new labor movement as well as employers and government lined up against nonwhites in the competition for industrial jobs. The American Federation of Labor excluded unskilled workers, women, most nonwhites, and foreigners. AFL President Samuel Gompers advocated racial purity in America, pitting white against nonwhite laborers and minorities against other minorities. The AFL was proud of the part it played in excluding Chinese and Japanese immigrants from these shores. Their cheap labor was a threat to the union members. Fear of job competition was also partially responsible for the rise of anti-Semitism and of anti-Catholicism as nationwide movements.

Economic crises at home led to ventures abroad. Unless new markets were found, warned a senator, "We shall have a revolution." Teddy Roosevelt said, "I should welcome almost any war, for I think this country needs one." In *1898* United States battleships and troops sallied forth into the Caribbean and Pacific. In ten weeks Spain was defeated and from Puerto Rico to the Philippines, the United States had gained an empire of rich islands and dark-skinned people. A Philippine drive for independence was crushed by a U.S. army of occupation with mass torture and murders. "Pitchfork" Ben Tillman of South Carolina did not miss the opportunity to ridicule his Senate colleagues from the North for hypocritically criticizing white Southerners who murdered Blacks, while they themselves slew Filipinos. Now, he said, "The

Introduction

North has a bloody shirt of its own. Many thousands of them have been made into shrouds for murdered Filipinos, done to death because they were fighting for liberty.''

In the turn-of-the-century era poverty was considered a sin and wealth a sign of heavenly favor. "Godliness is in league with riches," said William Lawrence, Episcopal bishop of Massachusetts. "To make money honestly is to preach the Gospel," announced Reverend Russell H. Conwell in his famous lecture "Acres of Diamonds." Business tycoon John D. Rockefeller said, "I am the trustee of the property of others, through the providence of God committed to my care."

Other than pious pronouncements, there was scant interest in the welfare of ordinary Americans. "The public be damned," said Cornelius Vanderbilt, millionaire businessman. "Society," announced Morton H. Smith, president of the Louisville and Nashville Railroad, was "created for the purpose of one man's getting what the other fellow has, if he can, and keep out of the penitentiary." Unethical manufacturers produced poisoned candies, diseased meats, and dangerous drugs. When a choking industrial smog blanketed the city of Chicago, a politician claimed its smoke was beneficial to children's lungs.

Human and natural resources had to surrender to the needs of the mighty. Entire forests fell before the axes of powerful lumber companies.

This, then, was America at the turn of the century—a country in turmoil, scarred by violence, racism, desperate poverty, and injustice.

Introduction

Traditionally, those who dominate a society dictate its chronicles, and this era was no exception. A way of life that existed for a few at the turn of the century has been offered as the story of an entire people. Thus, the myopic vision of the successful has replaced the truth. The history of the many remains to be told.

Where common people are mentioned at all in historical accounts, they are invariably commended for their devotion to duty and their capacity to endure and labor for the benefit of superiors. Their own thoughts and feelings, and their resilient spirit in the face of wretchedness, have been too often ignored.

Why have the poor, downtrodden, ordinary folk so infrequently been narrators of the past? Were they too busy? Too inarticulate? Too uninformed? Such undistinguished Americans, one might assume, faded without a trace into the obscurity that surrounded their lives.

Yet despite formidable handicaps, ordinary people *did* leave a written heritage. It is widely scattered, fragmented, and often incomplete, but it exists. People wrote letters to newspapers, unions, and one another. Some kept diaries and a few wrote books. Their words were recorded, often anonymously and with tantalizing brevity, by reporters, sociologists, and reformers. Without polish and elegance, these memoirs convey vast emotion and power. They have something to say, something history books generally leave out. Sometimes their unadorned words reveal much about the age itself, sometimes they give only a picture of the individual narrator.

The narratives collected here exhibit little tearful despondency. Despair leads to early graves, so people talked

Introduction

of hope, overcoming misfortune, and pushing ahead to seek answers. Yet among many, particularly nonwhites, fury smolders and occasionally bursts into flame.

Almost two hundred accounts of life by ordinary Amercans, ranging from short paragraphs to book-length autobiographies, were located in the research for this volume. The fourteen selections chosen cover a broad spectrum of American lives three-quarters of a century ago and appear with their original grammar and spelling.

The stories were chosen for their interest and for the picture they present of an emerging America. To accept this collection as a complete picture of the age or as the sole source of information would be wrong. It is, however, the raw material of an unrecognized heritage and deserves more than passing attention. Each account is a neglected and necessary ingredient of the whole—part of America's fascinating story.

MAKING OUR WAY

Sadie Frowne
A Sweatshop Girl at Sixteen

By the end of the nineteenth century the sweatshop was as much a fixed institution in urban America as the ghetto in which it was located. For young immigrant women, who had to spend as much time behind factory machines as in their homes, sweatshop labor was an experience they would never forget. Most sweatshops were located in dingy, dilapidated buildings. Operators were packed together without sufficient light or fresh air. The working day was long, the pay was a few dollars a week, and the rewards were few. Survival depended on satisfactions found outside working hours.

MAKING OUR WAY

Sadie Frowne's story is probably one which many other young European women could have told.

When I was a little more than ten years of age my father died. He was a good man and a steady worker, and we never knew what it was to be hungry while he lived. After he died troubles began, for the rent of our shop was about $6 a month and then there were food and clothes to provide. We needed little, it is true, but even soup, black bread, and onions we could not always get.

We struggled along till I was nearly thirteen years of age and quite handy at housework and shop keeping, so far as I could learn them there. But we fell behind in the rent and mother kept thinking more and more that we should have to leave Poland and go across the sea to America where we heard it was much easier to make money. Mother wrote to Aunt Fanny, who lived in New York, and told her how hard it was to live in Poland, and Aunt Fanny advised her to come and bring me. I was out at service at this time and mother thought she would leave me—as I had a good place—and come to this country alone, sending for me afterward. But Aunt Fanny would not hear of this. She said we should both come at once, and she went around among our relatives in New York and took up a subscription for our passage.

We came by steerage on a steamship in a very dark place that smelt dreadfully. There were hundreds of other people packed in with us, men, women, and children, and almost all of them were sick. It took us twelve days to

Sadie Frowne, A Sweatshop Girl at Sixteen

cross the sea, and we thought we should die, but at last the voyage was over, and we came up and saw the beautiful bay and the big woman with the spikes on her head and the lamp that is lighted at night in her hand (Goddess of Liberty).

Aunt Fanny and her husband met us at the gate of this country and were very good to us, and soon I had a place to live out (domestic servant), while my mother got work in a factory making white goods.

I was only a little over thirteen years of age and a greenhorn, so I received $9 a month and board and lodging, which I thought was doing well. Mother, who, as I have said, was very clever, made $9 a week on white goods, which means all sorts of underclothing, and is high class work.

But mother had a very gay disposition. She liked to go around and see everything, and friends took her about New York at night and she caught a bad cold and coughed and coughed. She really had hasty consumption, but she didn't know it, and I didn't know it, and she tried to keep on working, but it was no use. She had not the strength. Two doctors attended her, but they could do nothing, and at last she died and I was left alone. I had saved money while out at service, but mother's sickness and funeral swept it all away and now I had to begin all over again.

Aunt Fanny had always been anxious for me to get an education, as I did not know how to read or write, and she thought that was wrong. Schools are different in Poland from what they are in this country, and I was always too busy to learn to read and write. So when mother died I thought I would try to learn a trade and then I could go to school at night and learn to speak the English language well.

So I went to work in Allen Street (Manhattan) in what they call a sweatshop, making skirts by machine. I was new at the work and the foreman scolded me a great deal.

"Now, then," he would say, "this place is not for you to be looking around in. Attend to your work. That is what you have to do."

I did not know at first that you must not look around and talk, and I made many mistakes with the sewing, so that I was often called a "stupid animal." But I made $4 a week by working six days in the week. For there are two Sabbaths here—our own Sabbath, that comes on a Saturday, and the Christian Sabbath that comes on Sunday. It is against our law to work on our own Sabbath, so we work on their Sabbath.

In Poland I and my father and mother used to go to the synagogue on the Sabbath, but here the women don't go to the synagogue much, tho the men do. They are shut up working hard all the week long and when the Sabbath comes they like to sleep long in bed and afterward they must go out where they can breathe the air. The rabbis are strict here, but not so strict as in the old country.

I lived at this time with a girl named Ella, who worked in the same factory and made $5 a week. We had the room all to ourselves, paying $1.50 a week for it, and doing light housekeeping. It was in Allen Street and the window looked out of the back, which was good, because there was an elevated railroad in front, and in summertime a great deal of dust and dirt came in at the front windows. We were on the fourth story and could see all that was

Sadie Frowne, A Sweatshop Girl at Sixteen

going on in the back rooms of the houses behind us, and early in the morning the sun used to come in our window.

We did our cooking on an oil stove, and lived well, as this list of our expenses for one week will show:

Ella and Sadie for Food (One Week).

Tea	$0.06
Cocoa	.10
Bread and rolls	.40
Canned vegetables	.20
Potatoes	.10
Milk	.21
Fruit	.20
Butter	.15
Meat	.60
Fish	.15
Laundry	.25
Total	$2.42
Add rent	1.50
Grand total	$3.92

Of course, we could have lived cheaper, but we are both fond of good things and felt that we could afford them.

We paid *18* cents for a half pound of tea so as to get it good, and it lasted us three weeks, because we had cocoa for breakfast. We paid *5* cents for six rolls and *5* cents for a loaf of bread, which was the best quality. Oatmeal cost us *10* cents for three and one-half pounds, and we often had it in the morning, or Indian meal porridge in the place of it, costing about the same. Half a dozen eggs cost about *13* cents on an average, and we could get all the meat we wanted for a good hearty meal for *20* cents—two pounds of chops, or a steak, or a bit of veal, or a neck of lamb—something like that. Fish included butter fish, porgies, codfish, and smelts, averaging about *8* cents a pound.

Some people who buy at the last of the market, when the men with the carts want to go home, can get things very cheap, but they are likely to be stale, and we did not often do that with fish, fresh vegetables, fruit, milk, or meat. Things that kept well we did buy that way and got good bargains. I got thirty potatoes for *10* cents one time, tho generally I could not get more than *15* of them for that amount. Tomatoes, onions, and cabbages, too, we bought that way and did well, and we found a factory where we could buy the finest broken crackers for *3* cents a pound, and another place where we got broken candy for *10* cents a pound. Our cooking was done on an oil stove, and the oil for the stove and the lamp cost us *10* cents a week.

It cost me *$2* a week to live, and I had a dollar a week to spend on clothing and pleasure, and saved the other dollar. I went to night school, but it was hard work learning at first as I did not know much English.

Two years ago I came to this place, Brownsville, where so many of my people are, and where I have friends. I got work in a factory making underskirts—all sorts of cheap underskirts, like cotton and calico for the summer and woolen for the winter, but never the silk, satin, or velvet underskirts. I earned *$4.50* a week and lived on *$2* a week, the same as before.

I got a room in the house of some friends who lived

Sadie Frowne, A Sweatshop Girl at Sixteen

near the factory. I pay *$1* a week for the room and am allowed to do light housekeeping—that is, cook my meals in it. I get my own breakfast in the morning, just a cup of coffee and a roll, and at noontime I come home to dinner and take a plate of soup and a slice of bread with the lady of the house. My food for a week costs a dollar, just as it did in Allen Street, and I have the rest of my money to do as I like with. I am earning *$5.50* a week now, and will probably get another increase soon.

It isn't piecework in our factory, but one is paid by the amount of work done just the same. So it is like piecework. All the hands get different amounts, some as low as *$3.50* and some of the men as high as *$16* a week. The factory is in the third story of a brick building. It is in a room twenty feet long and fourteen broad. There are fourteen machines in it. I and the daughter of the people with whom I live work two of these machines. The other operators are all men, some young and some old.

At first a few of the young men were rude. When they passed me they would touch my hair and talk about my eyes and my red cheeks, and make jokes. I cried and said that if they did not stop I would leave the place. The boss said that that should not be, that no one must annoy me. Some of the other men stood up for me, especially Henry, who said two or three times that he wanted to fight. Now the men all treat me very nicely. It was just that some of them did not know better, not being educated.

Henry is tall and dark, and he has a small mustache. His eyes are brown and large. He is pale and much educated, having been to school. He knows a great many things and has some money saved. I think nearly *$400*. He is not going to be in a sweatshop all the time, but will soon be in the real estate business, for a lawyer that knows him well has promised to open an office and pay him to manage it.

Henry has seen me home every night for a long time and makes love to me. He wants me to marry him, but I am not seventeen yet, and I think that is too young. He is only nineteen, so we can wait.

I have been to the fortune teller's three or four times, and she always tells me that tho I have had such a lot of trouble I am to be very rich and happy. I believe her because she has told so many things that have come true. So I will keep on working in the factory for a time. Of course it is hard, but I would have to work hard even if I was married.

I get up at half-past five o'clock every morning and make myself a cup of coffee on the oil stove. I eat a bit of bread and perhaps some fruit and then go to work. Often I get there soon after six o'clock so as to be in good time, tho the factory does not open till seven. I have heard that there is a sort of clock that calls you at the very time you want to get up, but I can't believe that because I don't see how the clock would know.

At seven o'clock we all sit down to our machines and the boss brings to each one the pile of work that he or she is to finish during the day, what they call in English their "stint." This pile is put down beside the machine and as soon as a skirt is done it is laid on the other side of the machine. Sometimes the work is not all finished by six o'clock and then the one who is behind must work overtime. Sometimes one is finished ahead of time and

Sadie Frowne, A Sweatshop Girl at Sixteen

gets away at four or five o'clock, but generally we are not done till six o'clock.

The machines go like mad all day, because the faster you work the more money you get. Sometimes in my haste I get my finger caught and the needle goes right through it. It goes so quick, tho, that it does not hurt much. I bind the finger up with a piece of cotton and go on working. We all have accidents like that. Where the needle goes through the nail it makes a sore finger, or where it splinters a bone it does much harm. Sometimes a finger has to come off. Generally, tho, one can be cured by a salve.

All the time we are working the boss walks about examining the finished garments and making us do them over again if they are not just right. So we have to be careful as well as swift. But I am getting so good at the work that within a year I will be making *$7* a week, and then I can save at least *$3.50* a week. I have over *$200* saved now.

The machines are all run by foot power, and at the end of the day one feels so weak that there is a great temptation to lie right down and sleep. But you must go out and get air, and have some pleasure. So instead of lying down I go out, generally with Henry. Sometimes we go to Coney Island, where there are good dancing places, and sometimes we go to Ulmer Park to picnics. I am very fond of dancing, and, in fact, all sorts of pleasure. I go to the theater quite often, and like those plays that make you cry a great deal. "The Two Orphans" is good. Last time I saw it I cried all night because of the hard times that the children had in the play. I am going to see it again when it comes here.

§ *11* §

MAKING OUR WAY

For the last two winters I have been going to night school at Public School *84* on Glenmore Avenue. I have learned reading, writing, and arithmetic. I can read quite well in English now and I look at the newspapers every day. I read English books, too, sometimes. The last one that I read was "A Mad Marriage," by Charlotte Braeme. She's a grand writer and makes things just like real to you. You feel as if you were the poor girl yourself going to get married to a rich duke.

I am going back to night school again this winter. Plenty of my friends go there. Some of the women in my class are more than forty years of age. Like me, they did not have a chance to learn anything in the old country. It is good to have an education; it makes you feel higher. Ignorant people are all low. People say now that I am clever and fine in conversation.

We have just finished a strike in our business. It spread all over and the United Brotherhood of Garment Workers was in it. That takes in the cloakmakers, coatmakers, and all the others. We struck for shorter hours, and after being out four weeks won the fight. We only have to work nine and a half hours a day and we get the same pay as before. So the union does good after all in spite of what some people say against it—that it just takes our money and does nothing. I pay *25* cents a month to the union, but I do not begrudge that because it is for our benefit. The next strike is going to be for a raise of wages, which we all ought to have. But tho I belong to the union I am not a Socialist or an Anarchist. I don't know exactly what those things mean. There is a little expense for charity, too. If any worker is injured or sick we all give money to help.

Some of the women blame me very much because I spend so much money on clothes. They say that instead of a dollar a week I ought not to spend more than 25 cents a week on clothes, and that I should save the rest. But a girl must have clothes if she is to go into high society at Ulmer Park or Coney Island or the theater. Those who blame me are the old country people who have old-fashioned notions, but the people who have been here a long time know better. A girl who does not dress well is stuck in a corner, even if she is pretty, and Aunt Fanny says that I do just right to put on plenty of style.

I have many friends and we often have jolly parties. Many of the young men like to talk to me, but I don't go out with any except Henry.

Lately he has been urging me more and more to get married—but I think I'll wait.

Antanas Kaztaukis
From Lithuania
to the Chicago Stockyards

By 1893, when a mammoth Chicago fair celebrated the 400th anniversary of Columbus's arrival in America, that city had become a typical American metropolis. The population had grown from less than 30,000 in 1851 to over a million at the time of the Columbian Exposition. The vast majority of its inhabitants—seven out of ten—were foreign born. Most lived in crowded slums and worked hard at low-paying jobs. The city's 165 square miles roared with industrial activity. The noisy railroads and factory machinery and the pungent smells from the stockyards gave the city a unique character.

Antanas Kaztaukis, From Lithuania to Chicago

Among the thousands from abroad who poured into the city to find work was one who wrote the short memoir which follows. He used the pseudonym Antanas Kaztaukis because he feared the Russian government would punish his father and friend in Lithuania should he sign his real name.

A few years after the appearance of Antanas's story, Upton Sinclair published The Jungle, *an explosive exposé of immigrant labor exploitation in the meat-packing industry of Chicago. Based on nine months Sinclair spent with a European family recently arrived in the United States,* The Jungle *brought congressional passage of a Pure Food and Drug Act and sparked a greater interest in socialism.*

Antanas Kaztaukis offered no such utopian answer in his biography, but drew hope and inspiration from his ability to survive and from the purpose and comradeship he found in the trade union movement.

It was the shoemaker who made me want to come to America. He was a traveling shoemaker, for on our farms we tan our own cowhides, and the shoemaker came to make them into boots for us. By traveling he learned all the news and he smuggled in newspapers across the frontier from Germany. We were always glad to hear him talk.

I can never forget that evening four years ago. It was a cold December. We were in a big room in our log house in Lithuania. My good, kind, thin old mother sat near the wide fireplace, working her brown spinning wheel, with which she made cloth for our skirts and coats and pants. I sat on the floor in front of her with my knee-boots off and my feet stretched out to the fire. My father sat and smoked his pipe across the fireplace. Between was a kerosene lamp on a table, and under it sat the ugly shoemaker on a stool finishing a big yellow boot. I kept watching him. My fat, older brother, who sat behind with his fat wife, grinned and said: "Look out or your eyes will make holes in the leather." My brother's eyes were always dull and sleepy. Men like him stay in Lithuania.

At last the boot was finished. The little shoemaker held it up and looked at it.

"That's a good boot," said my father.

The shoemaker grunted. "That's a damn poor boot," he replied (instead of "damn" he said "skatina"), "a rough boot like all your boots, and so when you grow old you are lame. You have only poor things, for rich Russians get your good things, and yet you will not kick up against them. Bah!"

"I don't like your talk," said my father, and he spit into the fire, as he always did when he began to think. "I am honest. I work hard. We get along. That's all. So what good will such talk do me?"

"You!" cried the shoemaker, and he now threw the boot on the floor so that our big dog lifted up his head and looked around. "It's not you at all. It's the boy—that boy there!" and he pointed to me. "That boy must go to America!"

My mother looked frightened and she put her hand on my head. "No, no; he is only a boy," she said.

§ *16* §

"Bah!" cried the shoemaker. "He is eighteen and a man. You know where he must go in three years more."

We all knew he meant my five years in the army.

"Where is your oldest son? Dead. Oh, I know the Russians, they let him soak in rain, standing guard all night in the snow and ice he froze, the food was God's food, the vodka was cheap and rotten! Then he died."

He pulled out an old American newspaper, printed in the Lithuanian language, and I remembered he tore it he was so angry. "The world's good news is all kept away. We can only read what Russian officials print in their papers. Read? No, you can't read or write your own language, because there is no Lithuanian school—only the Russian school—[and] even those Russian schools make you pay to learn, and you have no money to pay. Will you never be ashamed—all you? Listen to me."

My fat brother grinned and said to the shoemaker, "You always stir up young men to go to America. Why don't you go yourself?"

"I am too old," he said, "to learn a new trade. These boots are no good in America. America is no place for us old rascals. My son is in Chicago in the stockyards, and he writes to me. They have hard knocks. If you are sick or old there and have no money you must die. That Chicago place has trouble, too. Do you see the light? That is kerosene. Do you remember the price went up last year? That is Rockefeller. My son writes me about him. He is another man wolf. A few men like him are grabbing all the good things—the oil and coal and meat and everything. But against these men you can strike if you are young. You can read free papers and prayer books. You can have free meetings and talk out what you think. And so if you are young you can change all these troubles. But I am old. I can feel it now, this winter. So I only tell young men to go." He looked hard at me and I looked at him.

He kept looking at me, but he opened the newspaper and held it up. "Someday," he said, "I will be caught and sent to jail, but I don't care. I got this from my son, who reads all he can find at night. It had to be smuggled in. I lend it many times to many young men. My son got it from the night school and he put it in Lithuanian for me to see." Then he bent over the paper a long time and his lips moved. At last he looked into the fire and fixed his hair, and then his voice was shaking and very low: " 'We know these are true things—that all men are born free and equal—that God gives them rights which no man can take away—that among these rights are life, liberty, and the getting of happiness.' "

He stopped, I remember, and looked at me, and I was not breathing. He said it again. " 'Life, liberty, and the getting of happiness.' Oh, that is what you want."

My mother began to cry. "He cannot go if his father commands him to stay," she kept saying. I knew this was true, for in Lithuania a father can command his son till he dies.

"No, he must not go," said the shoemaker, "if his father commands him to stay." He turned and looked hard at my father. My father was looking into the fire. In about five minutes the shoemaker got up and asked, "Well, what do you say—the army or America?" But my father shook his head and would not say anything.

After he was gone my father and I kept looking at the fire. My old mother stopped spinning and put her hand on my forehead.

"Alexandria is a fine girl," she whispered. This gave me a quick bad feeling. Alexandria was the girl I wanted to marry. She lived about ten miles away. Her father liked my father and they seemed to be glad that I loved her. My old mother kept her hands moving on my forehead. "Yes, she is a nice girl; a kind, beautiful girl," she kept whispering. We sat there till the lamp went out. Then the fire got low and the room was cold and we went to bed. But I could not sleep and kept thinking.

The next day my father told me that I could not go until the time came for the army, three years ahead. "Stay until then and then we will see," he said. My mother was very glad and so was I, because of Alexandria. But in the coldest part of that winter my dear old mother got sick and died.

That summer the shoemaker came again and talked with me. This time I was very eager to go to America, and my father told me I could go.

One morning I walked over to say good-by to Alexandria. When I saw her I felt very bad, and so did she. I had the strongest wish I ever had to take hold of her and keep her all my life. We stayed together till it was dark and night fogs came up out of the field grass, and we could hardly see the house. Then she said good-by. For many nights I kept remembering the way she looked up at me.

The next night after supper I started. It is against the law to sell tickets to America, but my father saw the secret agent in the village and he got a ticket from Germany and found us a guide. I had bread and cheese and honey and vodka and clothes in my bag. Some of the neighbors walked a few miles and said good-by and then went back. My father and my younger brother walked on all night with the guide and me. At daylight we came to the house of a man the guide knew. We slept there and that night I left my father and young brother. My father gave me $50 besides my ticket. The next morning before light we were going through the woods and we came to the frontier. Three roads run along the frontier. On the first road there is a soldier every mile, who stands there all night. On the second road is a soldier every half mile, and on the third road is a soldier every quarter of a mile. This guide went ahead through the woods. I hid with my big bag behind a bush and whenever he raised his hand I sneaked along. I felt cold all over and sometimes hot. He told me that sometimes he took twenty immigrants together, all without passports, and then he could not pass the soldiers and so he paid a soldier he knew one dollar a head to let them by. He said the soldier was very strict and counted them to see that he was not being cheated.

So I was in Germany. Two days after that we reached Tilzit and the guide took me to the railroad man. This man had a crowd of immigrants in a room, and we started that night on the railroad—fourth class. It was bad riding sometimes. I used to think of Alexandria. We were all green and slow. The railroad man used to say to me, "You will have to be quicker than this in Chicago," and he was right. We were very slow in the stations where we changed trains, and he used to shout at us then, and one old German man who spoke Lithuanian told me what the man was calling us. When he told me this I hurried, and so did the others, and we began to learn to be quicker. It took three days to get to Hamburg. There we were put in a big house called a barracks, and we waited a week. The old German man told me that the barracks men were cheating us. He had been once to Cincinnati in America to visit his son, who kept a saloon. His old, long pipe was stolen there. He kept saying, "Dem grafters, dem grafters," in a low voice whenever they brought food to sell, for our bags were now empty. They kept us there till our money was half spent on food. I asked the old man what kind of American men were grafters, and he said, "All kinds in Cincinnati, but more in Chicago!" I knew I was going to Chicago, and I began to think quicker. I thought quicker yet on the boat. I saw men playing cards. I played and lost $1.86 in my new money, till the old man came behind me and said, "Dem grafters." When I heard this I got scared and threw down my cards. That old man used to point up at the rich people looking down at us and say "Dem grafters." They were the richest people I had ever seen—the boat was the biggest boat I had ever seen—the machine that made it go was very big, and so was the horn that blew in a fog. I felt everything get bigger and go quicker every day.

It was the most when we came to New York. We were driven in a thick crowd to the railroad station. Everything got quicker—worse and worse—till then at last I was in a boarding house by the stockyards in Chicago, with three Lithuanians who knew my father's sisters at home.

MAKING OUR WAY

That first night we sat around in the house and they asked me, "Well, why did you come?" I told them about that first night and what the ugly shoemaker said about "life, liberty, and the getting of happiness." They all leaned back and laughed. "What you need is money," they said.

"It was all right at home. You wanted nothing. You ate your own meat and your own things on the farm. You made your own clothes and had your own leather. The other things you got at the Jew man's store and paid him with sacks of rye. But here you want a hundred things. Whenever you walk out you see new things you want, and you must have money to buy everything."

Then one man asked me, "How much have you?" and I told him *$30*. "You must buy clothes to look rich, even if you are not rich," he said. "With good clothes you will have friends."

The next morning three of these men took me to a store near the stockyards to buy a coat and pants. "Look out," said one of them. "Is he a grafter?" I asked. They all laughed. "You stand still. That is all you have to do," they said. So the Jew man kept putting on coats and I moved my arms and back and sides when they told me. We stayed there till it was time for dinner. Then we bought a suit. I paid *$5* and then I was to pay *$1* a week for five weeks.

In the afternoon I went to a big store. There was a man named Elias. "He is not a grafter," said my friends. He was nice to me and gave me good advice how to get a job. I bought two shirts, a hat, a collar, a necktie, two pairs of socks, and some shoes. We kept going upstairs

§ *22* §

and downstairs. I saw one Lithuanian man buying everything for his wife and three children, who would come here the next week from Lithuania. My things cost me $8. I put these on right away and then I began to feel better.

The next night they took me for a walk downtown. We would not pay to ride, so we walked so long that I wanted to take my shoes off, but I did not tell them this. When we came there I forgot my feet. We stood by one theater and watched for half an hour. Then we walked all around a store that filled one whole block and had walls of glass. Then we had a drink of whisky, and this is better than vodka. We felt happier and looked into *cafés*. We saw shiny carriages and automobiles. I saw men with dress suits, I saw women with such clothes that I could not think at all. Then my friends punched me and I turned around and saw one of these women, and with her was a gentleman in a fine dress suit. I began looking harder. It was the Jew man that sold me my suit. "He is a grafter," said my friends. "See what money can do." Then we walked home and I felt poor and my shoes got very bad.

That night I felt worse. We were tired out when we reached the stockyards, so we stopped on the bridge and looked into the river out there. It was so full of grease and dirt and sticks and boxes that it looked like a big, wide, dirty street, except in some places, where it boiled up. It made me sick to look at it. When I looked away I could see on one side some big fields full of holes, and these were the city dumps. On the other side were the stockyards, with twenty tall slaughter-house chimneys. The wind blew a big smell from them to us. Then we walked on between the yards and the dumps and all the houses looked bad and poor. In our house my room was in the basement. I lay down on the floor with three other men and the air was rotten. I did not go to sleep for a long time. I knew then that money was everything I needed. My money was almost gone and I thought that I would soon die unless I got a job, for this was not like home. Here money was everything and a man without money must die.

The next morning my friends woke me up at five o'clock and said, "Now, if you want life, liberty, and happiness," they laughed, "you must push for yourself. You must get a job. Come with us." And we went to the yards. Men and women were walking in by thousands as far as we could see. We went to the doors of one big slaughter house. There was a crowd of about 200 men waiting there for a job. They looked hungry and kept watching the door. At last a special policeman came out and began pointing to men, one by one. Each one jumped forward. Twenty-three were taken. Then they all went inside, and all the others turned their faces away and looked tired. I remember one boy sat down and cried, just next to me, on a pile of boards. Some policemen waved their clubs and we all walked on. I found some Lithuanians to talk with, who told me they had come every morning for three weeks. Soon we met other crowds coming away from other slaughter houses, and we all walked around and felt bad and tired and hungry.

That night I told my friends that I would not do this many days, but would go someplace else. "Where?"

they asked me, and I began to see then that I was in bad trouble, because I spoke no English. Then one man told me to give him $5 to give the special policeman. I did this and the next morning the policeman pointed me out, so I had a job. I have heard some big talk since then about my American freedom of contract, but I do not think I had much freedom in bargaining for this job with the Meat Trust. My job was in the cattle killing room. I pushed the blood along the gutter. Some people think these jobs make men bad. I do not think so. The men who do the killing are not as bad as the ladies with fine clothes who come every day to look at it, because they have to do it. The cattle do not suffer. They are knocked senseless with a big hammer and are dead before they wake up. This is done not to spare them pain, but because if they got hot and sweating with fear and pain the meat would not be so good. I soon saw that every job in the room was done like this—so as to save everything and make money. One Lithuanian who worked with me said, "They get all the blood out of those cattle and all the work out of us men." This was true, for we worked that first day from six in the morning till seven at night. The next day we worked from six in the morning till eight at night. The next day we had no work. So we had no good, regular hours. It was hot in the room that summer, and the hot blood made it worse.

I held this job six weeks and then I was turned off. I think some other man had paid for my job, or perhaps I was too slow. The foreman in that room wanted quick men to make the work rush, because he was paid more if the work was done cheaper and quicker. I saw now that every man was helping himself, always trying to get all the money he could. At that time I believed that all men in Chicago were grafters when they had to be. They only wanted to push themselves. Now, when I was idle I began to look about, and everywhere I saw sharp men beating out slow men like me. Even if we worked hard it did us no good. I had saved *$13: $5* a week for six weeks makes *$30,* and take off *$15* for six weeks' board and lodging and *$2* for other things. I showed this to a Lithuanian, who had been here two years, and he laughed. "It will be taken from you," he said. He had saved a hundred dollars once and had begun to buy a house on the installment plan, but something had happened that he did not know about and his landlord put him out and kept the hundred dollars. I found that many Lithuanians had been beaten this way. At home we never made a man sign contract papers. We only had him make the sign of a cross and promise he would do what he said. But this was no good in Chicago. So these sharp men were beating us.

I saw this, too, in the newspaper. I was beginning to learn English, and at night in the boarding house the men who did not play cards used to read the paper to us. The biggest word was "graft" in red letters on the front page. Another word was "trust." This paper kept putting these two words together. Then I began to see how every American man was trying to get money for himself. I wondered if the old German man in Cincinnati had found his pipe yet. I felt very bad and sorrowful in that month. I kept walking around with many other Lithuanians who had no job. Our money was going and we could find nothing to do. At night we got homesick for our fine green mountains. We read all the news about home in our Lithuanian Chicago newspaper, *The Katalikas*. It is a good paper and gives all the news. In the same office we bought this song, which was written in Brooklyn by P. Brandukas. He, too, was homesick. It is sung all over Chicago now and you can hear it in the summer evenings through the open windows. In English it is something like this:

> *Oh, Lithuania, so dear to me,*
> *Good-by to you, my Fatherland.*
> *Sorrowful in my heart I leave you,*
> *I know not who will stay to guard you.*
>
> *Is it enough for me to live and enjoy between*
>   *my neighbors,*
> *In the woods with the flowers and birds?*
> *Is it enough for me to live peaceful between*
>   *my friends?*
> *No, I must go away from my old father and mother.*
>
> *The sun shines bright,*
> *The flowers smell sweet.*
> *The birds are singing,*
> *They make the country glad;*
> *But I cannot sing because I must leave you.*

Those were bad days and nights. At last I had a chance to help myself. Summer was over and Election Day was coming. The Republican boss in our district, Jonidas, was a saloonkeeper. A friend took me there. Jonidas shook hands and treated me fine. He taught me to sign my name, and the next week I went with him to an office and signed some paper, and then I could vote. I voted as I was told, and then they got me back into the yards to work, because one big politician owns stock in one of those houses. Then I felt that I was getting in beside the game. I was in a combine like other sharp men. Even when work was slack I was all right, because they got me a job in the street-cleaning department. I felt proud, and I went to the back room in Jonidas's saloon and got him to write a letter to Alexandria to tell her she must come soon and be my wife.

But this was just the trouble. All of us were telling our friends to come soon. Soon they came—even thousands. The employers in the yard liked this, because those sharp foremen are inventing new machines and the work is easier to learn, and so these slow Lithuanians and even green girls can learn to do it, and then the Americans and Germans and Irish are put out and the employer saves money, because the Lithuanians work cheaper. This was why the American labor unions began to organize us all just the same as they had organized the Bohemians and Poles before us.

Well, we were glad to be organized. We had learned that in Chicago every man must push himself always, and Jonidas had taught us how much better we could push ourselves by getting into a combine. Now, we saw that this union was the best combine for us, because it was the only combine that could say, "It is our business to raise your wages."

But that Jonidas—he spoiled our first union. He was sharp. First he got us to hire the room over his saloon.

He used to come in at our meetings and sit in the back seat and grin. There was an Irishman there from the union headquarters, and he was trying to teach us to run ourselves. He talked to a Lithuanian, and the Lithuanian said it to us, but we were slow to do things, and we were jealous and were always jumping up to shout and fight. So the Irishman used to wipe his hot red face and call us bad names. He told the Lithuanian not to say these names to us, but Jonidas heard them, and in his saloon, where we all went down after the meeting when the Irishman was gone, Jonidas gave us free drinks and then told us the names. I will not write them here.

One night that Irishman did not come and Jonidas saw his chance and took the chair. He talked very fine and we elected him president. We made him treasurer, too. Down in the saloon he gave us free drinks and told us we must break away from the Irish grafters. The next week he made us strike, all by himself. We met twice a day in the saloon and spent all of our money on drinks and then the strike was over. I got out of this union after that. I had been working hard in the cattle killing room and I had a better job. I was called a cattle butcher now and I joined the Cattle Butchers' Union. This union is honest and it has done me a great deal of good.

It has raised my wages. The man who worked at my job before the union came was getting through the year an average of $9 a week. I am getting $11. In my first job I got $5 a week. The man who works there now gets $5.75.

It has given me more time to learn to read and speak

and enjoy life like an American. I never work now from 6 A.M. to 9 P.M. and then be idle the next day. I work now from 7 A.M. to 5:30 P.M., and there are not so many idle days. The work is evened up.

With more time and more money I live much better and I am very happy. So is Alexandria. She came a year ago and has learned to speak English already. Some of the women go to the big store the day they get here, when they have not even sense to pick out the clothes that look right, but Alexandria waited three weeks till she knew, and so now she looks the finest of any woman in the district. We have four nice rooms, which she keeps very clean, and she has flowers growing in boxes in the two front windows. We do not go much to church, because the church seems to be too slow. But we belong to a Lithuanian society that gives two picnics in summer and two big balls in winter, where we have a fine time. I go one night a week to the Lithuanian Concertina Club. On Sundays we go on the trolley out into the country.

But we like to stay at home more now because we have a baby. When he grows up I will not send him to the Lithuanian Catholic school. They have only two bad rooms and two priests, who teach only in Lithuanian from prayer books. I will send him to the American school, which is very big and good. The teachers there are Americans and they belong to the Teachers' Labor Union, which has three thousand teachers and belongs to our Chicago Federation of Labor. I am sure that such teachers will give him a good chance.

Our union sent a committee to Springfield last year

and they passed a law which prevents boys and girls below sixteen from working in the stockyards.

We are trying to make the employers pay on Saturday night in cash. Now they pay in checks and the men have to get money the same night to buy things for Sunday, and the saloons cash checks by thousands. You have to take one drink to have the check cashed. It is hard to take one drink.

The union is doing another good thing. It is combining all the nationalities. The night I joined the Cattle Butchers' Union I was led into the room by a Negro member. With me were Bohemians, Germans, and Poles, and Mike Donnelly, the president, is an Irishman. He spoke to us in English and then three interpreters told us what he said. We swore to be loyal to our union above everything else except the country, the city and the state—to be faithful to each other—to protect the women workers—to do our best to understand the history of the labor movement, and to do all we could to help it on. Since then I have gone there every two weeks and I help the movement by being an interpreter for the other Lithuanians who come in. That is why I have learned to speak and write good English. The others do not need me long. They soon learn English, too, and when they have done that they are quickly becoming Americans.

But the best thing the union does is to make me feel more independent. I do not have to pay to get a job and I cannot be discharged unless I am no good. For almost the whole *30,000* men and women are organized now in some one of our unions and they all are directed by our central council. No man knows what it means to be sure of his job unless he has been fired like I was once without any reason being given.

So this is why I joined the labor union. There are many better stories than mine, for my story is very common. There are thousands of immigrants like me. Over *300,000* immigrants have been organized in the last three years by the American Federation of Labor. The immigrants are glad to be organized if the leaders are as honest as Mike Donnelly is. You must get money to live well and to get money you must combine. I cannot bargain alone with the Meat Trust. I tried it and it does not work.

My young brother came over three weeks ago, to escape being sent out to fight in Japan. I tried to have my father come, too, but he was too old. I wish that ugly little shoemaker would come. He would make a good walking delegate.

An Anonymous Farmer's Wife

Americans have always celebrated those who work close to the soil as being "close to God." The man who produces the nation's crops has been a hero to generations, a sturdy bulwark of morality, hard work, and stamina. Yet farmers' wives have rarely received their due. They worked alongside their husbands in the field and then returned to take care of home and children. They too helped build a nation and seldom had time to enjoy the fruits of their labors.

How heavy their load really was and how they felt about it has often escaped the attention of historians.

That is why this autobiography of an anonymous farmer's wife is so instructive. Her work schedule, incredibly burdensome, monotonous, and unending, was typical. One suspects that her artistic interests were far from typical. And despite her enormous contribution to the success of the farm, her part of the marital relationship required her to dutifully accept her husband's commands, no matter how strongly opposed her own inclinations might be.

I have been a farmer's wife in one of the states of the Middle West for thirteen years, and everybody knows that the farmer's wife must of a necessity be a very practical woman, if she would be a successful one.

I am not a practical woman and consequently have been accounted a failure by practical friends and especially by my husband, who is wholly practical.

We are told that the mating of people of opposite natures promotes intellectuality in the offspring; but I think that happy homes are of more consequence than extreme precocity of children. However, I believe that people who are thinking of mating do not even consider whether it is to be the one or the other.

We do know that when people of opposite tastes get married there's a discordant note runs through their married life. It's only a question of which one has the stronger will in determining which taste shall predominate.

In our case my husband has the stronger will; he is

innocent of book learning, is a natural hustler who believes that the only way to make an honest living lies in digging it out of the ground, so to speak, and being a farmer, he finds plenty of digging to do; he has an inherited tendency to be miserly, loves money for its own sake rather than for its purchasing power, and when he has it in his possession he is loath to part with it, even for the most necessary articles, and prefers to eschew hired help in every possible instance that what he does make may be his very own.

No man can run a farm without someone to help him, and in this case I have always been called upon and expected to help do anything that a man would be expected to do; I began this when we were first married, when there were few household duties and no reasonable excuse for refusing to help.

I was reared on a farm, was healthy and strong, was ambitious, and the work was not disagreeable, and having no children for the first six years of married life, the habit of going whenever asked to became firmly fixed, and he had no thought of hiring a man to help him, since I could do anything for which he needed help.

I was an apt student at school and before I was eighteen I had earned a teacher's certificate of the second grade and would gladly have remained in school a few more years, but I had, unwittingly, agreed to marry the man who is now my husband, and tho I begged to be released, his will was so much the stronger that I was unable to free myself without wounding a loving heart, and could not find it in my heart to do so.

All through life I have found my dislike for giving

offense to be my undoing. When we were married and moved away from my home church, I fain would have adopted the church of my new residence, but my husband did not like to go to church; had rather go visiting on Sundays, and, rather than have my right hand give offense, I cut it off.

I always had a passion for reading; during girlhood it was along educational lines; in young womanhood it was for love stories, which remained ungratified because my father thought it sinful to read stories of any kind, and especially love stories.

Later, when I was married, I borrowed everything I could find in the line of novels and stories, and read them by stealth still, for my husband thought it a willful waste of time to read anything and that it showed a lack of love for him if I would rather read than to talk to him when I had a few moments of leisure, and, in order to avoid giving offense and still gratify my desire, I would only read when he was not at the house, thereby greatly curtailing my already too limited reading hours.

In reading miscellaneously I got glimpses now and then of the great poets and authors, which aroused a great desire for a thorough perusal of them all; but up till the present time I have not been permitted to satisfy this desire. As the years have rolled on there has been more work and less leisure until it is only by the greatest effort that I may read current news.

It is only during the last three years that I have had the news to read, for my husband is so very penurious that he would never consent to subscribing for papers of any kind and that old habit of avoiding that which would give offense was so fixed that I did not dare to break it.

The addition of two children to our family never altered or interfered with the established order of things to any appreciable extent. My strenuous outdoor life agreed with me, and even when my children were born I was splendidly prepared for the ordeal and made rapid recovery. I still hoed and tended the truck patches and garden, still watered the stock and put out feed for them, still went to the hay field and helped harvest and house the bounteous crops; still helped harvest the golden grain later on when the cereals ripened; often took one team and dragged ground to prepare the seed-bed for wheat for weeks at the time, while my husband was using the other team on another farm which he owns several miles away.

While the children were babies they were left at the house, and when they were larger they would go with me to my work; now they are large enough to help a little during the summer and to go to school in winter; they help a great deal during the fruit canning season—in fact, can and do work at almost everything, pretty much as I do.

All the season, from the coming in of the first fruits until the making of mincemeat at Christmastime, I put up canned goods for future use; gather in many bushels of field beans and the other crops usually raised on the farm; make sourkraut, ketchup, pickles, etc.

This is a vague, general idea of how I spend my time; my work is so varied that it would be difficult, indeed, to describe a typical day's work.

Any bright morning in the latter part of May I am out of bed at four o'clock; next, after I have dressed and combed my hair, I start a fire in the kitchen stove, and while the stove is getting hot I go to my flower garden and gather a choice, half-blown rose and a spray of bride's wreath, and arrange them in my hair, and sweep the floors and then cook breakfast.

While the other members of the family are eating breakfast I strain away the morning's milk (for my husband milks the cows while I get breakfast), and fill my husband's dinner-pail, for he will go to work on our other farm for the day.

By this time it is half-past five o'clock, my husband is gone to his work, and the stock loudly pleading to be turned into the pastures. The younger cattle, a half dozen steers, are left in the pasture at night, and I now drive the two cows a half-quarter mile and turn them in with the others, come back, and then there's a horse in the barn that belongs in a field where there is no water, which I take to a spring quite a distance from the barn; bring it back and turn it into a field with the sheep, a dozen in number, which are housed at night.

The young calves are then turned out into the warm sunshine, and the stock hogs, which are kept in a pen, are clamoring for food, and I carry a pailful of swill to them, and hasten to the house and turn out the chickens and put out feed and water for them, and it is, perhaps, *6:30* A.M.

I have not eaten breakfast yet, but that can wait; I make the beds next and straighten things up in the living room, for I dislike to have the early morning caller

An Anonymous Farmer's Wife

find my house topsy-turvy. When this is done I go to the kitchen, which also serves as a dining room, and uncover the table, and take a mouthful of food occasionally as I pass to and fro at my work until my appetite is appeased.

By the time the work is done in the kitchen it is about *7:15* A.M., and the cool morning hours have flown, and no hoeing done in the garden yet, and the children's toilet has to be attended to and churning has to be done.

Finally the children are washed and churning done, and it is eight o'clock, and the sun getting hot, but no matter, weeds die quickly when cut down in the heat of the day, and I use the hoe to a good advantage until the dinner hour, which is *11:30* A.M. We come in, and I comb my hair, and put fresh flowers in it, and eat a cold dinner, put out feed and water for the chickens; set a hen, perhaps, sweep the floors again; sit down and rest, and read a few moments, and it is nearly one o'clock, and I sweep the door yard while I am waiting for the clock to strike the hour.

I make and sow a flower bed, dig around some shrubbery, and go back to the garden to hoe until time to do the chores at night, but ere long some hogs come up to the back gate, through the wheat field, and when I go to see what is wrong I find that the cows have torn the fence down, and they, too, are in the wheat field.

With much difficulty I get them back into their own domain and repair the fence. I hoe in the garden till four o'clock; then I go into the house and get supper, and prepare something for the dinner-pail tomorrow; when supper is all ready it is set aside, and I pull a few hundred plants of tomato, sweet potato or cabbage for transplanting, set them in a cool, moist place where they will not wilt, and I then go after the horse, water him, and put him in the barn; call the sheep and house them, and go after the cows and milk them, feed the hogs, put down hay for three horses, and put oats and corn in their troughs, and set those plants and come in and fasten up the chickens, and it is dark. By this time it is *8* o'clock P.M.; my husband has come home, and we are eating supper; when we are through eating I make the beds ready, and the children and their father go to bed, and I wash the dishes and get things in shape to get breakfast quickly next morning.

It is now about *9* o'clock P.M., and after a short prayer I retire for the night.

As a matter of course, there's hardly two days together which require the same routine, yet every day is as fully occupied in some way or other as this one, with varying tasks as the seasons change. In early spring we are planting potatoes, making plant beds, planting garden, early corn patches, setting strawberries, planting corn, melons, cow peas, sugar cane, beans, popcorn, peanuts, etc.

Oats are sown in March and April, but I do not help do that, because the ground is too cold.

Later in June we harvest clover hay, in July timothy hay, and in August pea hay.

Winter wheat is ready to harvest the latter part of June, and oats the middle of July.

These are the main crops, supplemented by cabbages, melons, potatoes, tomatoes, etc.

An Anonymous Farmer's Wife

Fully half of my time is devoted to helping my husband, more than half during the active work season, and not that much during the winter months; only a very small portion of my time is devoted to reading. My reading matter accumulates during the week, and I think I will stay at home on Sunday and read, but as we have many visitors on Sunday I am generally disappointed.

I sometimes visit my friends on Sunday because they are so insistent that I should, tho I would prefer spending the day reading quietly at home. I have never had a vacation, but if I should be allowed one I should certainly be pleased to spend it in an art gallery.

As winter draws nigh I make snug all the vegetables and apples, pumpkins, and such things as would damage by being frozen, and gather in the various kinds of nuts which grow in our woods, to eat during the long, cold winter.

My husband's work keeps him away from home during the day all the winter, except in extremely inclement weather, and I feed and water the stock, which have been brought in off the pastures; milk the cows and do all the chores which are to be done about a farm in winter.

By getting up early and hustling around pretty lively I do all this and countless other things; keep house in a crude, simple manner; wash, make, and mend our clothes; make rag carpets, cultivate and keep more flowers than anybody in the neighborhood, raise some chickens to sell and some to keep, and even teach instrumental music sometimes.

I have always had an itching to write, and with all my

multitudinous cares, I have written, in a fitful way, for several papers, which do not pay for such matter, just because I was pleased to see my articles in print.

I have a long list of correspondents, who write regularly and often to me, and, by hook and crook, I keep up with my letter-writing, for, next to reading, I love to write and receive letters, tho my husband says I will break him up buying so much writing material; when, as a matter of course, I pay for it out of my own scanty income.

I am proud of my children, and have, from the time they were young babies, tried to make model children of them. They were not spoiled as some babies are, and their education was begun when I first began to speak to them, with the idea of not having the work to do over later on. True, they did not learn to spell until they were old enough to start to school, because I did not have time to teach them that; but, in going about my work, I told them stories of all kinds, in plain, simple language which they could understand, and after once hearing a story they could repeat it in their own way, which did not differ greatly from mine, to anyone who cared to listen, for they were not timid or afraid of anybody.

I have watched them closely, and never have missed an opportunity to correct their errors until their language is as correct as that of the average adult, as far as their vocabulary goes, and I have tried to make it as exhaustive as my time would permit.

I must admit that there is very little time for the higher life for myself, but my soul cries out for it, and my heart is not in my homely duties; they are done in a mechanical, abstracted way, not worthy of a woman of high ambitions; but my ambitions are along other lines.

I do not mean to say that I have no ambition to do my work well, and to be a model housekeeper, for I would scorn to slight my work intentionally; it is just this way: There are so many outdoor duties that the time left for household duties is so limited that I must rush through them, with a view to getting each one done in the shortest possible time, in order to get as many things accomplished as possible, for there is never time to do half as much as needs to be done.

All the time that I have been going about this work I have been thinking of things I have read; of things I have on hand to read when I can get time, and of other things which I have a desire to read, but cannot hope to while the present condition exists.

As a natural consequence, there are, daily, numerous instances of absent-mindedness on my part; many things left undone that I really could have done, by leaving off something else of less importance, if I had not forgotten the thing of the more importance. My husband never fails to remind me that it is caused by my reading so much; that I would get along much better if I should never see a book or paper, while really I would be distracted if all reading matter was taken from me.

I use an old-fashioned churn, and the process of churning occupies from thirty minutes to three hours, according to the condition of the cream, and I always read something while churning, and tho that may look like a poor way to attain self-culture, yet if your reading is of the nature to bring about that desirable result, one will surely be greatly benefited by these daily exercises.

But if one is just reading for amusement, they might read a great deal more than that and not derive any benefit; but my reading has always been for the purpose of becoming well informed; and when knitting stockings for the family I always have a book or paper in reading distance; or, if I have a moment to rest or to wait on something, I pick up something and read during the time. I even take a paper with me to the fields and read while I stop for rest.

I often hear ladies remark that they do not have time to read. I happen to know that they have a great deal more time than I do, but not having any burning desire to read, the time is spent in some other way; often spent at a neighbor's house gossiping about the other neighbors.

I suppose it is impossible for a woman to do her best at everything which she would like to do, but I really would like to. I almost cut sleep out of my routine in trying to keep up all the rows which I have started in on; in the short winter days I just get the cooking and house straightening done in addition to looking after the stock and poultry, and make a garment occasionally, and wash and iron the clothes; all the other work is done after night by lamplight, and when the work for the day is over, or at least the most pressing part of it, and the family are all asleep and no one to forbid it, I spend a few hours writing or reading.

The minister who performed the marriage ceremony for us has always taken a kindly interest in our fortunes and, knowing of my literary bent, has urged me to turn it to account; but there seemed to be so little time and opportunity that I could not think seriously of it, altho I longed for a literary career; but my education had been dropped for a dozen years or more, and I knew that I was not properly equipped for that kind of a venture.

This friend was so insistent that I was induced to compete for a prize in a short story contest in a popular magazine not long since, tho I entered it fully prepared for a failure.

About that time there came in my way the literature of a correspondence school which would teach, among other things, short story writing by mail. The school has proven very trustworthy, and I am in the midst of a course of instruction which is very pleasing to me; and I find time for study and exercise between the hours of eight and eleven at night, when the family are asleep and quiet. I am instructed to read a great deal, with a certain purpose in view, but that is impossible, since I had to promise my husband that I would drop all my papers, periodicals, etc., on which I was paying out money for subscription before he would consent to my taking the course. This I felt willing to do, that I might prepare myself for more congenial tasks; I hope to accomplish something worthy of note in a literary way since I have been a failure in all other pursuits.

My friends have always been so kind as not to hint that I had not come up to their expectations in various lines, but I inwardly knew that they regarded me as a financial failure; they knew that my husband would not allow the money that was made off the farm to be spent on the family, but still they knew of other men who did the same, yet the wives managed some way to have money of their own and to keep up the family expenses and clothe themselves and children nicely anyhow, but they did not seem to take into account that these thrifty wives had the time all for their own in which to earn a livelihood while my time was demanded by my husband, to be spent in doing things for him which would contribute to the general proceeds of the farm, yet would add nothing to my income, since I was supposed to look to my own resources for my spending money.

When critical housewives spend the day with me I always feel that my surroundings appear to a disadvantage. They cannot possibly know the inside workings of our home, and knowing myself to be capable of the proper management of a home if I had the chance of others, I feel like I am receiving a mental criticism from them which is unmerited, and when these smart neighbors tell me proudly how many young chicks they have, and how many eggs and old hens they have sold during the year, I am made to feel that they are crowing over their shrewdness, which they regard as lacking in me, because they will persist in measuring my opportunities by their own.

I might add that the neighbors among whom I live are illiterate and unmusical, and that my redeeming qualities, in their eyes, are my superior education and musical abilities; they are kind enough to give me more than justice on these qualities because they are poor judges of such matters.

But money is king, and if I might turn my literary

bent to account, and surround myself with the evidences of prosperity, I may yet hope fully to redeem myself in their eyes, and I know that I will have attained my ambition in that line.

Rocco Corresca
Bootblack

Millions of Italians came to live in America around the turn of the century; more than two million came during the decade that ended in 1900. For many the countryside symbolized the oppression they had known in the old country, so they chose to live in cities. They crowded together near relatives or those from their region. Asked where they intended to settle, hundreds of thousands told American immigration authorities "Mulberry Street," the heart of New York City's Little Italy.

Though they came with a dream of quick wealth, most found they had exchanged one set of squalid circum-

Rocco Corresca, Bootblack

stances for another. They struggled to learn a new language, new ways, and to find the promised opportunities. Starting at the bottom, they slowly made their way up, some faster than others. The story of Rocco Corresca may not be a "rags to riches" tale, but at nineteen he had learned a great deal and was on his way to success.

When I was a very small boy I lived in Italy in a large house with many other small boys, who were all dressed alike and were taken care of by some nuns. It was a good place, situated on the side of the mountain, where grapes were growing and melons and oranges and plums.

They taught us our letters and how to pray and say the catechism, and we worked in the fields during the middle of the day. We always had enough to eat and good beds to sleep in at night, and sometimes there were feast days, when we marched about wearing flowers.

Those were good times and they lasted till I was nearly eight years of age. Then an old man came and said he was my grandfather. He showed some papers and cried over me and said that the money had come at last and now he could take me to his beautiful home. He seemed very glad to see me and after they looked at his papers he took me away and we went to the big city—Naples. He kept talking about his beautiful house, but when we got there it was a dark cellar that he lived in and I did not like it at all. Very rich people were on the first floor. They had carriages and servants and music and plenty of good things to eat, but we were down below in the cellar and had nothing. There were four other boys in the cellar and the old man said they were all my brothers. All were larger than I and they beat me at first till one day Francisco said that they should not beat me any more, and then Paulo, who was the largest of all, fought him till Francisco drew a knife and gave him a cut. Then Paulo, too, got a knife and said that he would kill Francisco, but the old man knocked them both down with a stick and took their knives away and gave them beatings.

Each morning we boys all went out to beg and we begged all day near the churches and at night near the theaters, running to the carriages and opening the doors and then getting in the way of the people so that they had to give us money or walk over us. The old man often watched us and at night he took all the money except when we could hide something.

It was very hard in the wintertime for we had no shoes and we shivered a great deal. The old man said that we were no good, that we were ruining him, that we did not bring in enough money. He told me that I was fat and that people would not give money to fat beggars. He beat me, too, because I didn't like to steal, as I had heard it was wrong.

"Ah!" said he, "that is what they taught you at that place, is it? To disobey your grandfather that fought with Garibaldi! That is a fine religion!"

The others all stole as well as begged, but I didn't like it and Francisco didn't like it either.

Then the old man said to me: "If you don't want to be a thief you can be a cripple. That is an easy life and they make a great deal of money."

Rocco Corresca, Bootblack

I was frightened then, and that night I heard him talking to one of the men that came to see him. He asked how much he would charge to make me a good cripple like those that crawl about the church. They had a dispute, but at last they agreed and the man said that I should be made so that people would shudder and give me plenty of money.

I was much frightened, but I did not make a sound and in the morning I went out to beg with Francisco. I said to him: "I am going to run away. I don't believe Tony is my grandfather. I don't believe that he fought for Garibaldi, and I don't want to be a cripple, no matter how much money the people may give."

"Where will you go?" Francisco asked me.

"I don't know," I said; "somewhere."

He thought awhile and then he said: "I will go, too."

So we ran away out of the city and begged from the country people as we went along. We came to a village down by the sea and a long way from Naples and there we found some fishermen and they took us aboard their boat. We were with them five years, and tho it was a very hard life we liked it well because there was always plenty to eat. Fish do not keep long and those that we did not sell we ate.

The chief fisherman, whose name was Ciguciano, had a daughter, Teresa, who was very beautiful, and tho she was two years younger than I, she could cook and keep house quite well. She was a kind, good girl and he was a good man. When we told him about the old man who told us he was our grandfather, the fisherman said he was an old rascal who should be in prison for life. Teresa cried much when she heard that he was going to make me a cripple. Ciguciano said that all the old man had taught us was wrong—that it was bad to beg, to steal, and to tell lies. He called in the priest and the priest said the same thing and was very angry at the old man in Naples, and he taught us to read and write in the evenings. He also taught us our duties to the church and said that the saints were good and would only help men to do good things, and that it was a wonder that lightning from heaven had not struck the old man dead when he knocked down the saint's figure.

We grew large and strong with the fisherman and he told us that we were getting too big for him, that he could not afford to pay us the money that we were worth. He was a fine, honest man—one in a thousand.

Now and then I had heard things about America—that it was a far off country where everybody was rich and that Italians went there and made plenty of money, so that they could return to Italy and live in pleasure ever after. One day I met a young man who pulled out a handful of gold and told me he had made that in America in a few days.

I said that I should like to go there, and he told me that if I went he would take care of me and see that I was safe. I told Francisco and he wanted to go, too. So we said good-by to our good friends. Teresa cried and kissed us both, and the priest came and shook our hands and told us to be good men, and that no matter where we went God and his saints were always near us and that if we lived well we should all meet again in heaven. We cried, too, for it was our home, that place. Ciguciano gave us money and slapped us on the back and said that we should be great. But he felt bad, too, at seeing us go away after all that time.

The young man took us to a big ship and got us work away down where the fires are. We had to carry coal to the place where it could be thrown on the fires. Francisco and I were very sick from the great heat at first and lay on the coal for a long time, but they threw water on us and made us get up. We could not stand on our feet well, for everything was going around and we had no strength. We said that we wished we had stayed in Italy no matter how much gold there was in America. We could not eat for three days and could not do much work. Then we got better and sometimes we went up above and looked about. There was no land anywhere and we were much surprised. How could the people tell where to go when there was no land to steer by?

We were so long on the water that we began to think we should never get to America or that, perhaps, there was not any such place, but at last we saw land and came up to New York.

We were glad to get over without giving money, but I have heard since that we should have been paid for our work among the coal and that the young man who had sent us got money for it. We were all landed on an island and the bosses there said that Francisco and I must go back because we had not enough money, but a man named Bartolo came up and told them that we were brothers and he was our uncle and would take care of us. He brought two other men who swore that they knew us in Italy and that Bartolo was our uncle. I had never seen any of them before, but even then Bartolo might be my uncle, so I did not say anything. The bosses of the island let us go out with Bartolo after he had made the oath.

We came to Brooklyn to a wooden house in Adams Street that was full of Italians from Naples. Bartolo had a room on the third floor and there were fifteen men in the room, all boarding with Bartolo. He did the cooking on a stove in the middle of the room and there were beds all around the sides, one bed above another. It was very hot in the room, but we were soon asleep, for we were very tired.

The next morning, early, Bartolo told us to go out and pick rags and get bottles. He gave us bags and hooks and showed us the ash barrels. On the streets where the fine houses are the people are very careless and put out good things, like mattresses and umbrellas, clothes, hats, and boots. We brought all these to Bartolo and he made them new again and sold them on the sidewalk; but mostly we brought rags and bones. The rags we had to wash in the backyard and then we hung them to dry on lines under the ceiling in our room. The bones we kept under the beds till Bartolo could find a man to buy them.

Most of the men in our room worked at digging the sewer. Bartolo got them the work and they paid him about one quarter of their wages. Then he charged them for board and he bought the clothes for them, too. So they got little money after all.

Bartolo was always saying that the rent of the room

was so high that he could not make anything, but he was really making plenty. He was what they call a padrone and is now a very rich man. The men that were living with him had just come to the country and could not speak English. They had all been sent by the young man we met in Italy. Bartolo told us all that we must work for him and that if we did not the police would come and put us in prison.

He gave us very little money, and our clothes were some of those that were found on the street. Still we had enough to eat and we had meat quite often, which we never had in Italy. Bartolo got it from the butcher—the meat that he could not sell to the other people—but it was quite good meat. Bartolo cooked it in the pan while we all sat on our beds in the evening. Then he cut it into small bits and passed the pan around, saying:

"See what I do for you and yet you are not glad. I am too kind a man, that is why I am so poor."

We were with Bartolo nearly a year, but some of our countrymen who had been in the place a long time said that Bartolo had no right to us and we could get work for a dollar and a half a day, which, when you make it *lire* (reckoned in the Italian currency) is very much. So we went away one day to Newark and got work on the street. Bartolo came after us and made a great noise, but the boss said that if he did not go away soon the police would have him. Then he went, saying that there was no justice in this country.

We paid a man five dollars each for getting us the work and we were with that boss for six months. He was Irish, but a good man and he gave us our money every Saturday night. We lived much better than with Bartolo, and when the work was done we each had nearly $200 saved. Plenty of the men spoke English and they taught us, and we taught them to read and write. That was at night, for we had a lamp in our room, and there were only five other men who lived in that room with us.

We got up at half-past five o'clock every morning and made coffee on the stove and had a breakfast of bread and cheese, onions, garlic, and red herrings. We went to work at seven o'clock and in the middle of the day we had soup and bread in a place where we got it for two cents a plate. In the evenings we had a good dinner with meat of some kind and potatoes. We got from the butcher the meat that other people would not buy because they said it was old, but they don't know what is good. We paid four or five cents a pound for it and it was the best, tho I have heard of people paying sixteen cents a pound.

When the Newark boss told us that there was no more work Francisco and I talked about what we would do and we went back to Brooklyn to a saloon near Hamilton Ferry, where we got a job cleaning it out and slept in a little room upstairs. There was a bootblack named Michael on the corner and when I had time I helped him and learned the business. Francisco cooked the lunch in the saloon and he, too, worked for the bootblack and we were soon able to make the best polish.

Then we thought we would go into business and we got a basement on Hamilton Avenue, near the ferry, and put four chairs in it. We paid $75 for the chairs and all the other things. We had tables and looking glasses there and curtains. We took the papers that have the pictures in and made the place high toned. Outside we had a big sign that said

THE BEST SHINE FOR TEN CENTS

Men that did not want to pay ten cents could get a good shine for five cents, but it was not an oil shine. We had two boys helping us and paid each of them fifty cents a day. The rent of the place was *$20* a month, so the expenses were very great, but we made money from the beginning. We slept in the basement, but got our meals in the saloon till we could put a stove in our place, and then Francisco cooked for us all. That would not do, tho, because some of our customers said that they did not like to smell garlic and onions and red herrings. I thought that was strange, but we had to do what the customers said. So we got the woman who lived upstairs to give us our meals and paid her *$1.50* a week each. She gave the boys soup in the middle of the day—five cents for two plates.

We remembered the priest, the friend of Ciguciano, and what he had said to us about religion, and as soon as we came to the country we began to go to the Italian church. The priest we found here was a good man, but he asked the people for money for the church. The Italians did not like to give because they said it looked like buying religion. The priest says it is different here from Italy because all the churches there are what they call endowed, while here all they have is what the people give. Of course I and Francisco understand that, but the Italians who cannot read and write shake their hands and say that it is wrong for a priest to want money.

We had said that when we saved *$1,000* each we would go back to Italy and buy a farm, but now that the time is coming we are so busy and making so much money that we think we will stay. We have opened another parlor near South Ferry, in New York. We have to pay *$30* a month rent, but the business is very good. The boys in this place charge sixty cents a day because there is so much work.

At first we did not know much of this country, but by and by we learned. There are here plenty of Protestants who are heretics, but they have a religion, too. Many of the finest churches are Protestant, but they have no saints and no altars, which seems strange.

These people are without a king such as ours in Italy. It is what they call a Republic, as Garibaldi wanted, and every year in the fall the people vote. They wanted us to vote last fall, but we did not. A man came and said that he would get us made Americans for fifty cents and then we could get two dollars for our votes. I talked to some of our people and they told me that we should have to put a paper in a box telling who we wanted to govern us.

I went with five men to the court and when they asked me how long I had been in the country I told them two years. Afterward my countrymen said I was a fool and would never learn politics. "You should have said you were five years here and then we would swear to it," was what they told me.

There are two kinds of people that vote here, Republicans and Democrats. I went to a Republican meeting and the man said that the Republicans want a Republic and the Democrats are against it. He said that Democrats are for a king whose name is [William Jennings] Bryan and who is an Irishman. There are some good Irishmen, but many of them insult Italians. They call us Dagoes. So I will be a Republican.

I like this country now and I don't see why we should have a king. Garibaldi didn't want a king and he was the greatest man that ever lived.

I and Francisco are to be Americans in three years. The court gave us papers and said we must wait and we must be able to read some things and tell who the ruler of the country is.

There are plenty of rich Italians here, men who a few years ago had nothing and now have so much money that they could not count all their dollars in a week. The richest ones go away from the other Italians and live with the Americans.

We have joined a club and have much pleasure in the evenings. The club has rooms down in Sackett Street and we meet many people and are learning new things all the time. We were very ignorant when we came here, but now we have learned much.

On Sundays we get a horse and carriage from the grocer and go down to Coney Island. We go to the theaters often and other evenings we go to the houses of our friends and play cards.

I am nineteen years of age now and have *$700* saved. Francisco is twenty-one and has about *$900*. We shall open some more parlors soon. I know an Italian who was a bootblack ten years ago and now bosses bootblacks all over the city, who has so much money that if it was turned into gold it would weigh more than himself.

Francisco and I have a room to ourselves now and some people call us "swells." Francisco bought a gold watch with a gold chain as thick as his thumb. He is a very handsome fellow and I think he likes a young lady that he met at a picnic out at Ridgewood.

I often think of Ciguciano and Teresa. He is a good man, one in a thousand, and she was very beautiful. Maybe I shall write to them about coming to this country.

An Anonymous Georgia Sharecropper

~~~~

For the Black people of the South—about one-third of the region's population—life changed very little with the end of slavery. Their new freedom meant that they were no longer owned by individual whites. However, they were subject to rule by the white community as a whole and abuse by any individual. The system of Southern justice, education, public welfare and just about everything else was run by whites. Segregation was rigidly enforced, and white power over Blacks extended far beyond economic, political, and legal spheres. A vast and complicated social code made Black men, women, and children subject to *white whims and white pleasures.*

The basis of this new slavery was the sharecropper system that bound most Blacks to land owned by whites. Debts to the landlord kept Blacks in peonage, unable to leave the job or move away. The story of this Georgia peon and his wife, dictated to a magazine writer who put it into a form suitable for publication, shows their lives were not their own, nor did they have any rights whites felt obliged to respect.

I am a negro and was born some time during the war in Elbert County, Ga., and I reckon by this time I must be a little over forty years old. My mother was not married when I was born, and I never knew who my father was or anything about him. Shortly after the war my mother died, and I was left to the care of my uncle. All this happened before I was eight years old, and so I can't remember very much about it. When I was about ten years old my uncle hired me out to Captain ———. I had already learned how to plow, and was also a good hand at picking cotton. I was told that the Captain wanted me for his houseboy, and that later on he was going to train me to be his coachman. To be a coachman in those days was considered a post of honor, and, young as I was, I was glad of the chance. But I had not been at the Captain's a month before I was put to work on the farm, with some twenty or thirty other negroes—men, women, and children. From the beginning the boys had the same tasks as the men and women. There was no difference. We all worked hard during the week and would frolic on Saturday nights and often on Sundays. And everybody was happy. The men got $3 a week and the women $2. I don't know what the children got. Every week my uncle collected my money for me, but it was very little of it that I ever saw. My uncle fed and clothed me, gave me a place to sleep, and allowed me ten or fifteen cents a week for "spending change," as he called it. I must have been seventeen or eighteen years old before I got tired of that arrangement, and felt that I was man enough to be working for myself and handling my own wages. The other boys about my age and size were "drawing" their own pay, and they used to laugh at me and call me "Baby" because my old uncle was always on hand to "draw" my pay. Worked up by these things, I made a break for liberty. Unknown to my uncle or the Captain I went off to a neighboring plantation and hired myself out to another man. The new landlord agreed to give me forty cents a day and furnish me one meal. I thought that was doing fine. Bright and early one Monday morning I started for work, still not letting the others know anything about it. But they found it out before sundown. The Captain came over to the new place and brought some kind of officer of the law. The officer pulled out a long piece of paper from his pocket and read it to my new employer. When this was done I heard my new boss say:

"I beg your pardon, Captain. I didn't know this nigger was bound out to you, or I wouldn't have hired him."

"He certainly is bound out to me," said the Captain. "He belongs to me until he is twenty-one, and I'm going to make him know his place."

MAKING OUR WAY

So I was carried back to the Captain's. That night he made me strip off my clothing down to my waist, had me tied to a tree in his backyard, ordered his foreman to give me thirty lashes with a buggy whip across my bare back, and stood by until it was done. After that experience the Captain made me stay on his place night and day—but my uncle still continued to "draw" my money.

I was a man nearly grown before I knew how to count from one to one hundred. I was a man nearly grown before I ever saw a colored schoolteacher. I never went to school a day in my life. Today I can't write my own name, though I can read a little. I was a man nearly grown before I ever rode on a railroad train, and then I went on an excursion from Elberton to Athens. What was true of me was true of hundreds of other negroes around me—'way off there in the country, fifteen or twenty miles from the nearest town.

When I reached twenty-one the Captain told me I was a free man, but he urged me to stay with him. He said he would treat me right, and pay me as much as anybody else would. The Captain's son and I were about the same age, and the Captain said that, as he had owned my mother and uncle during slavery, and as his son didn't want me to leave them (since I had been with them so long), he wanted me to stay with the old family. And I stayed. I signed a contract—that is, I made my mark—for one year. The Captain was to give me *$3.50* a week, and furnish me a little house on the plantation—a one-room log cabin similar to those used by his other laborers.

During that year I married Mandy. For several years Mandy had been the house-servant for the Captain, his wife, his son, and his three daughters, and they all seemed to think a good deal of her. As an evidence of their regard they gave us a suit of furniture, which cost about $25, and we set up housekeeping in one of the Captain's two-room shanties. I thought I was the biggest man in Georgia. Mandy still kept her place in the "Big House" after our marriage. We did so well for the first year that I renewed my contract for the second year, and for the third, fourth, and fifth year I did the same thing. Before the end of the fifth year the Captain had died, and his son, who had married some two or three years before, took charge of the plantation. Also, for two or three years, this son had been serving at Atlanta in some big office to which he had been elected. I think it was in the Legislature or something of that sort—anyhow, all the people called him Senator. At the end of the fifth year the Senator suggested that I sign up a contract for ten years; then, he said, we wouldn't have to fix up papers every year. I asked my wife about it; she consented; and so I made a ten-year contract.

Not long afterward the Senator had a long, low shanty built on his place. A great big chimney, with a wide, open fireplace, was built at one end of it, and on each side of the house, running lengthwise, there was a row of frames or stalls just large enough to hold a single mattress. The places for these mattresses were fixed one above the other; so that there was a double row of these stalls or pens on each side. They looked for all the world like stalls for horses. Since then I have seen cabooses similarly arranged as sleeping quarters for railroad laborers. Nobody seemed to know what the Senator was fixing for. All doubts were put aside one bright day in April when about forty able-bodied negroes, bound in iron chains, and some of them handcuffed, were brought out to the Senator's farm in three big wagons. They were quartered in the long, low shanty, and it was afterward called the stockade. This was the beginning of the Senator's convict camp. These men were prisoners who had been leased by the Senator from the State of Georgia at about *$200* each per year, the state agreeing to pay for guards and physicians, for necessary inspection, for inquests, all rewards for escaped convicts, the costs of litigation, and all other incidental camp expenses. When I saw these men in shackles, and the guards with their guns, I was scared nearly to death. I felt like running away, but I didn't know where to go. And if there had been anyplace to go to, I would have had to leave my wife and child behind. We free laborers held a meeting. We all wanted to quit. We sent a man to tell the Senator about it. Word came back that we were all under contract for ten years and that the Senator would hold us to the letter of the contract, or put us in chains and lock us up—the same as the other prisoners. It was made plain to us by some white people we talked to that in the contracts we had signed we had all agreed to be locked up in a stockade at night or at any other time that our employer saw fit; further, we learned that we could not lawfully break our contract for any reason and go and hire ourselves to somebody else without the consent of our employer; and more than that, if we got mad and ran away, we could be run down by bloodhounds, arrested without process of law, and be returned to our employer, who, according to the contract, might beat us brutally or administer any other kind of punishment that he thought proper. In other words, we had sold ourselves into slavery—and what could we do about it? The white folks had all the courts, all the guns, all the hounds, all the railroads, all the telegraph wires, all the newspapers, all the money, and nearly all the land—and we had only our ignorance, our poverty, and our empty hands. We decided that the best thing to do was to shut our mouths, say nothing, and go back to work. And most of us worked side by side with those convicts during the remainder of the ten years.

But this first batch of convicts was only the beginning. Within six months another stockade was built, and twenty or thirty other convicts were brought to the plantation, among them six or eight women! The Senator had bought an additional thousand acres of land, and to his already large cotton plantation he added two great sawmills and went into the lumber business. Within two years the Senator had in all nearly *200* negroes working on his plantation—about half of them free laborers, so-called, and about half of them convicts. The only difference between the free laborers and the others was that the free laborers could come and go as they pleased at night—that is, they were not locked up at night, and were not, as a general thing, whipped for slight offenses.

The troubles of the free laborers began at the close of the ten-year period. To a man, they all wanted to quit when the time was up. To a man, they all refused to sign new contracts—even for one year, not to say anything of ten years. And just when we thought that our bondage was at an end we found that it had really just begun. Two or three years before, or about a year and a half after the Senator had started his camp, he had established a large store, which was called the commissary. All of us free laborers were compelled to buy our supplies—food, clothing, etc.—from that store. We never used any money in our dealings with the commissary, only tickets or orders, and we had a general settlement once each year, in October. In this store we were charged all sorts of high prices for goods, because every year we would come out in debt to our employer. If not that, we seldom had more than *$5* or *$10* coming to us—and that for a whole year's work. Well, at the close of the tenth year, when we kicked and meant to leave the Senator, he said to some of us with a smile (and I never will forget that smile—I can see it now):

"Boys, I'm sorry you're going to leave me. I hope you will do well in your new places—so well that you will be able to pay me the little balances which most of you owe me."

Word was sent out for all of us to meet him at the commissary at two o'clock. There he told us that, after we had signed what he called a written acknowledgment of our debts, we might go and look for new places. The storekeeper took us one by one and read to us statements of our accounts. According to the books there was no man of us who owed the Senator less than *$100;* some of us were put down for as much as *$200.* I owed *$165,* according to the bookkeeper. These debts were not accumulated during one year, but ran back for three and four years, so we were told—in spite of the fact that we understood that we had had a full settlement at the end of each year.

An Anonymous Georgia Sharecropper

But no one of us would have dared to dispute a white man's word—oh, no; not in those days. Besides, we fellows didn't care anything about the amounts—we were after getting away; and we had been told that we might go, if we signed the acknowledgments. We would have signed anything, just to get away. So we stepped up, we did, and made our marks.

That same night we were rounded up by a constable and ten or twelve white men, who aided him, and we were locked up, every one of us, in one of the Senator's stockades. The next morning it was explained to us by the two guards appointed to watch us that, in the papers we had signed the day before, we had not only made the acknowledgment of our indebtedness, but that we had also agreed to work for the Senator until the debts were paid by hard labor. And from that day forward we were treated just like convicts. Really we had made ourselves lifetime slaves, or peons, as the laws called us. But, call it slavery, peonage, or what not, the truth is we lived in a hell on earth what time we spent in the Senator's peon camp.

I lived in that camp, as a peon, for nearly three years. My wife fared better than I did, as did the wives of some of the other negroes, because the white men about the camp used these unfortunate creatures as their mistresses. When I was first put in the stockade my wife was still kept for a while in the "Big House," but my little boy, who was only nine years old, was given away to a negro family across the river in South Carolina, and I never saw or heard of him after that. When I left the camp my wife had had two children for some one of the white bosses, and she was living in fairly good shape in a little house off to herself. But the poor negro women who were not in the class with my wife fared about as bad as the helpless negro men. Most of the time the women who were peons or convicts were compelled to wear men's clothes. Sometimes, when I have seen them dressed like men, and plowing or hoeing or hauling logs or working at the blacksmith's trade, just the same as men, my heart would bleed and my blood would boil, but I was powerless to raise a hand. It would have meant death on the spot to have said a word. Of the first six women brought to the camp, two of them gave birth to children after they had been there more than twelve months—and the babies had white men for their fathers!

The stockades in which we slept were, I believe, the filthiest places in the world. They were cesspools of nastiness. During the thirteen years that I was there I am willing to swear that a mattress was never moved after it had been brought there, except to turn it over once or twice a month. No sheets were used, only dark-colored blankets. Most of the men slept every night in the clothing that they had worked in all day. Some of the worst characters were made to sleep in chains. The doors were locked and barred each night, and tallow candles were the only lights allowed. Really the stockades were but little more than cow lots, horse stables, or hog pens. Strange to say, not a great number of these people died while I was there, tho a great many came away maimed and bruised and, in some cases, disabled for life. As far as I remember only about ten died during the last ten years that I was there, two of these being killed outright by the guards for trivial offenses.

It was a hard school that peon camp was, but I learned more there in a few short months by contact with those poor fellows from the outside world than ever I had known before. Most of what I learned was evil, and I now know that I should have been better off without the knowledge, but much of what I learned was helpful to me. Barring two or three severe and brutal whippings which I received, I got along very well, all things considered; but the system is damnable. A favorite way of whipping a man was to strap him down to a log, flat on his back, and spank him fifty or sixty times on his bare feet with a shingle or a huge piece of plank. When the man would get up with sore and blistered feet and an aching body, if he could not then keep up with the other men at work he would be strapped to the log again, this time face downward, and would be lashed with a buggy trace on his bare back. When a woman had to be whipped it was usually done in private, tho they would be compelled to fall down across a barrel or something of the kind and receive the licks on their backsides.

The working day on a peon farm begins with sunrise and ends when the sun goes down; or, in other words, the average peon works from ten to twelve hours each day, with one hour (from twelve o'clock to one o'clock) for dinner. Hot or cold, sun or rain, this is the rule. As to their meals, the laborers are divided up into squads or companies, just the same as soldiers in a great military camp would be. Two or three men in each stockade are appointed as cooks. From thirty to forty men report to each cook. In the warm months (or eight or nine months out of the year) the cooking is done on the outside, just behind the stockades; in the cold months the cooking is done inside the stockades. Each peon is provided with a great big tin cup, a flat tin pan, and two big tin spoons. No knives or forks are ever seen, except those used by the cooks. At mealtime the peons pass in single file before the cooks and hold out their pans and cups to receive their allowances. Cow peas (red or white, which when boiled turn black), fat bacon, and old-fashioned Georgia cornbread, baked in pones from one to two and three inches thick, make up the chief articles of food. Black coffee, black molasses, and brown sugar are also used abundantly. Once in a great while, on Sundays, biscuits would be made, but they would always be made from the kind of flour called "shorts." As a rule, breakfast consisted of coffee, fried bacon, cornbread, and sometimes molasses—and one "helping" of each was all that was allowed. Peas, boiled with huge hunks of fat bacon, and a hoe-cake, as big as a man's hand, usually answered for dinner. Sometimes this dinner bill of fare gave place to bacon and greens (collard or turnip) and pot liquor. Tho we raised corn, potatoes and other vegetables, we never got a chance at such things unless we could steal them and cook them secretly. Supper consisted of coffee, fried bacon, and molasses. But, altho the food was limited to certain things, I am sure we all got a plenty of the things allowed. As coarse as these things were, we kept, as a rule, fat and sleek and as strong as mules. And that, too, in spite of the fact that we had no special arrangements for taking regular baths, and no very great effort was made to keep us regularly in clean clothes. No tables were used or allowed. In summer we would sit down on the ground and eat our meals, and in winter we would sit around inside the filthy stockades. Each man was his own dishwasher—that is to say, each man was responsible for the care of his pan and cup and spoons. My dishes got washed about once a week!

Today, I am told, there are six or seven of these private camps in Georgia—that is to say, camps where most of the convicts are leased from the State of Georgia. But there are hundreds and hundreds of farms all over the state where negroes, and in some cases poor white folks, are held in bondage on the ground that they are working out debts, or where the contracts which they have made hold them in a kind of perpetual bondage, because, under those contracts, they may not quit one employer and hire out to another, except by and with the knowledge and consent of the former employer. One of the usual ways to secure laborers for a large peonage camp is for the proprietor to send out an agent to the little courts in the towns and villages, and where a man charged with some petty offense has no friends or money the agent will urge him to plead guilty, with the understanding that the agent will pay his fine, and in that way save him from the disgrace of being sent to jail or the chain gang! For this high favor the man must sign beforehand a paper signifying his willingness to go to the farm and work out the amount of the fine imposed. When he reaches the farm he has to be fed and clothed, to be sure, and these things are charged up to his account. By the time he has worked out his first debt another is hanging over his head, and so on and so on, by a sort of endless chain, for an indefinite period, as in every case the indebtedness is arbitrarily arranged by the employer. In many cases it is very evident that the court officials are in collusion with the proprietors or agents, and that they divide the "graft" among themselves. As an example of this dickering among the whites, every year many convicts were brought to the Senator's camp from a certain county in south Georgia, 'way down in the turpentine district. The majority of these men were charged with adultery, which is an offense against the laws of the great and sovereign State of Georgia! Upon inquiry I learned that down in that county a number of negro lewd women were employed by certain white men to entice negro men into their houses; and then, on certain nights, at a given signal, when all was in readiness, raids would be made by the officers upon these houses, and the men would be arrested and charged with living in adultery. Nine out of ten of these men, so arrested and so charged, would find their way ultimately to some convict camp, and, as I said, many of them found their way every year to the Senator's camp while I was there. The low-down women were never punished in any way. On the contrary, I was told that they always seemed to stand in high favor with the sheriffs, constables, and other officers. There can be no room to doubt that they assisted very materially in furnishing laborers for the prison pens of Georgia, and the belief was general among the men that they were regularly paid for their work. I could tell more, but I've said enough to make anybody's heart sick. I am glad that the federal au-

An Anonymous Georgia Sharecropper

thorities are taking a hand in breaking up this great and terrible iniquity. It is, I know, widespread throughout Georgia and many other southern states. Since Judge Speer fired into the gang last November at Savannah, I notice that arrests have been made of seven men in three different sections of the state—all charged with holding men in peonage. Somewhere, somehow, a beginning of the end should be made.

But I didn't tell you how I got out. I didn't get out—they put me out. When I had served as a peon for nearly three years—and you remember that they claimed that I owed them only *$165*—when I had served for nearly three years, one of the bosses came to me and said that my time was up. He happened to be the one who was said to be living with my wife. He gave me a new suit of overalls, which cost about seventy-five cents, took me in a buggy and carried me across the Broad River into South Carolina, set me down and told me to "git." I didn't have a cent of money, and I wasn't feeling well, but somehow I managed to get a move on me. I begged my way to Columbia. In two or three days I ran across a man looking for laborers to carry to Birmingham, and I joined his gang. I have been here in the Birmingham district since they released me, and I reckon I'll die either in a coal mine or an iron furnace. It don't make much difference which. Either is better than a Georgia peon camp. And a Georgia peon camp is hell itself!

An Anonymous Irish Cook

Supported by unshakable religious faith and close family ties, the millions of Irish immigrants who arrived early in the nineteenth century carried with them little more than a willingness to work and a few stitches of clothing. Protestants soon convinced themselves that America had opened the gates to its first white "enemy from within." Fleeing famine, oppression, and internal strife at home, the newcomers were hardly prepared for or interested in upsetting the social order. Thousands died on the nightmare voyage across the Atlantic, and the survivors left the gangplank desperate to recuperate, to find a home

An Anonymous Irish Cook

and a job. In crowded slums, they found scant welcome, except from their own kind.

Men and youths were soon at work constructing canals, roads, sewers, tunnels, and railroads and later digging in mines or working in factories. Women who could leave their large families found jobs cleaning, in domestic service, and in industry. The Irish were thrust into competition with free Blacks for the least skilled, most undesirable and lowest paid positions; in the South they were often considered more expendable than slaves. Poor health, malnutrition, and industrial accidents took their toll, and there was often not enough work to go around. By the 1850s the Irish third of New York City's population made up 69 percent of the paupers and 55 percent of those arrested.

Because they were poor, usually from rural areas, unskilled, uneducated, and particularly because they were the first large Catholic migration, the Irish were viewed with a mixture of loathing and fear. The Know-Nothings, charging "The Negro is black outside; the Irishman is black inside," claimed they were part of a Papist conspiracy to bring down democratic institutions. Anti-Catholic propaganda became a thriving industry. In the 1890s the American Protective Association renewed fears of "Papists" by claiming Irish domination of city politics and pollution of representative government.

However, because of mounting numbers, urban Irish were beginning by then to command some political power with its accompanying economic advances. These changes from early to later nineteenth century are reflected in the reminiscences of an immigrant woman who rose from *house servant to cook to owner of her own boarding house. Taken down by her former employer, identified only as "one of the best known literary women of America," her memoir was published, dialect intact, in 1905.*

I don't know why anybody wants to hear my history. Nothing ever happened to me worth the tellin' except when my mother died. . . . I was born nigh to Limavaddy; it's a pretty town close to Londonderry. We lived in a peat cabin, but it had a good thatched roof. Mother put on that roof. It isn't a woman's work, but she—was able for it.

There were sivin childher of us. John an' Matthew they went to Australia. Mother was layin' by for five year to get their passage money. They went into the bush. We heard twice from thim and then no more. Not another word and that is forty year gone now—on account of them not reading and writing. Learning isn't cheap in them old countries as it is here, you see. I suppose they're dead now—John would be ninety now—and in heaven. They were honest men. My mother sent Joseph to Londonderry to larn the weaver's trade. My father he never was a steddy worker. He took to the drink early in life. My mother an' me an' Tilly we worked in the field for Squire Varney. Yes, plowin' an' seedin' and diggin'—any farm work he'd give us. We did men's work, but we didn't get men's pay. No, of course not. In winter we did lace work for a merchant in Londonderry. (Ann still can embroider beautifully.) It was pleasanter nor diggin'

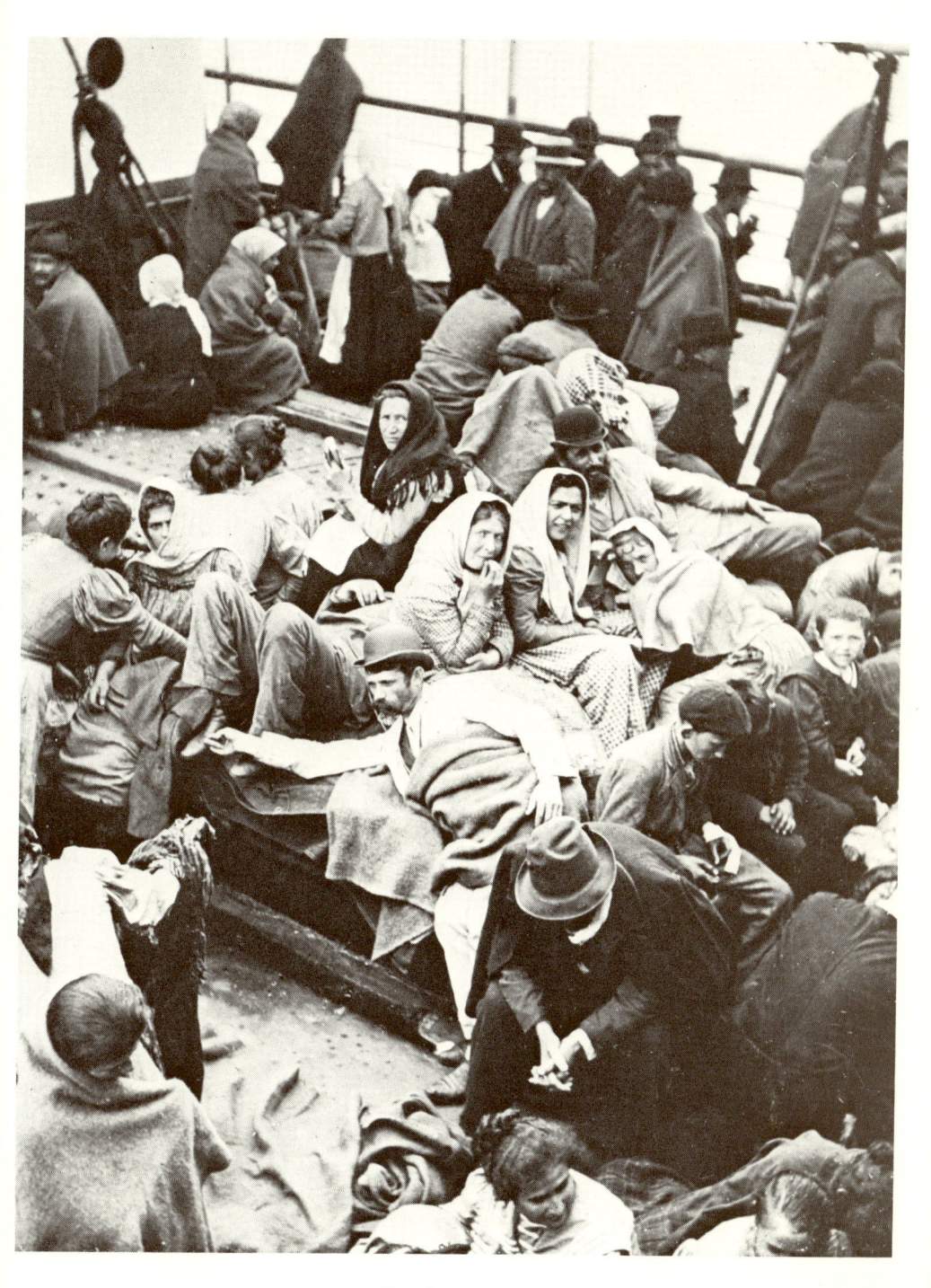

Immigrants coming to America, the "Land of Promise"

Arriving at Ellis Island

Overcrowded tenements housed the poor.

At home under the dump on New York's Rivington Street

Life in the city was a constant struggle to survive. Members of New York's 20th Precinct police force

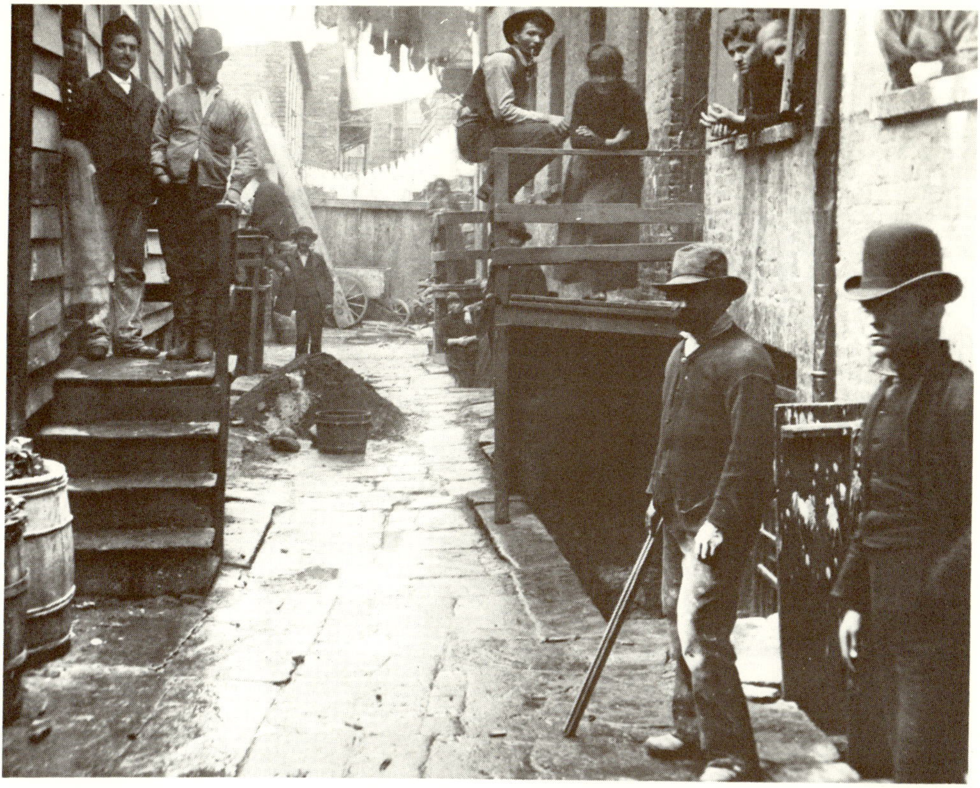

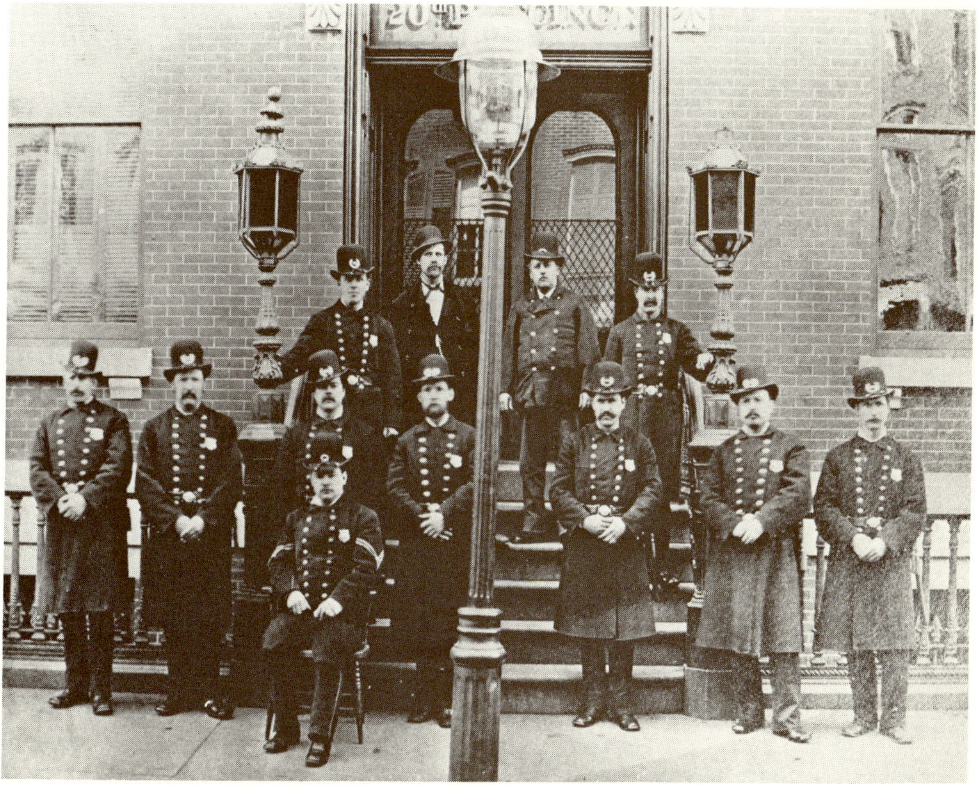
20th

Young children worked long hours in factories.

Garment workers labor in a crowded sweatshop.

Indian boys at a government boarding school

An Anonymous Irish Cook

after my hands was fit for it. But it took two weeks every year to clean and soften my hands for the needle.

Pay was very small and the twins—that was Maria and Philip—they were too young to work at all. What did we eat? Well, just potatoes. On Sundays, once a month, we'd maybe have a bit of flitch [cured pork]. When the potatoes rotted—that was the hard times! Oh, yes, I mind the famine years. An' the cornmeal that the 'Mericans sent. The folk said they'd rather starve nor eat it. We didn't know how to cook it. Here I eat corn dodgers and fried mush fast enough.

Maria—she was one of the twins—she died the famine year of the typhus and—well, she sickened of the herbs and roots we eat—we had no potatoes.

Mother said when Maria died, "There's a curse on ould green Ireland and we'll get out of it." So we worked an' saved for four year an' then Squire Varney helped a bit an' we sent Tilly to America. She had always more head than me. She came to Philadelphia and got a place for general housework at Mrs. Bent's. Tilly got but two dollars a week, bein' a greenhorn. But she larned hand over hand, and Mrs. Bent kept no other help and laid out to teach her. She larned her to cook and bake and to wash and do up shirts—all American fashion. Then Tilly axed three dollars a week. Mother always said, "Don't ax a penny more than you're worth. But know your own vally and ax that."

She had no expenses and laid by money enough to bring me out before the year was gone. I sailed from Londonderry. The ship was a sailin' vessel, the "Mary Jane." The passage was $12. You brought your own eating, your tea an' meal, an' most had flitch. There was two big stoves that we cooked on. The steerage was a dirty place and we were eight weeks on the voyage—overtime three weeks. The food ran scarce, I tell you, but the captain gave some to us, and them that had plenty was kind to the others. I've heard bad stories of things that went on in the steerage in them old times—smallpox and fevers and starvation and worse. But I saw nothing of them in my ship. The folks were decent and the captain was kind.

When I got here Mrs. Bent let Tilly keep me for two months to teach me—me bein' such a greenhorn. Of course I worked for her. Mr. Bent was foreman then in Spangler's big mills. After two months I got a place. They were nice appearing people enough, but the second day I found out they were Jews. I never had seen a Jew before, so I packed my bag and said to the lady, "I beg your pardon, ma'am, but I can't eat the bread of them as crucified the Saviour." "But," she said, "he was a Jew." So at that I put out. I couldn't hear such talk.

Then I got a place for general housework with Mrs. Carr. I got $2 till I learned to cook good, and then $3 and then $4. I was in that house as cook and nurse for twenty-two years. Tilly lived with the Bents till she died, eighteen years. Mr. Bent came to be partner in the mills and got rich, and they moved into a big house in Germantown and kept a lot of help and Tilly was housekeeper. How did we keep our places so long? Well, I think me and Tilly was clean in our work and we was decent, and, of course, we was honest. Nobody living can say that one of the McNabbs ever wronged him of a cent. Mrs. Carr's interests was my interests. I took better care of her things than she did herself, and I loved the childher as if they was my own. She used to tell me my sin was I was stingy. I don't know. The McNabbs are no wasteful folk. I've worn one dress nine year and it looked decent then. Me and Tilly saved till we brought Joseph and Phil over, and they went into Mr. Bent's mills as weaver and spool boy and then they saved, and we all brought out my mother and father. We rented a little house in Kensington for them. There was a parlor in it and kitchen and two bedrooms and bathroom and marble doorstep, and a bell. We paid nine dollars a month rent. You'd pay double that now. It took all our savings to furnish it, but Mrs. Bent and Mrs. Carr gave us lots of things to go in. To think of mother having a parlor and marble steps and a bell! They came on the old steamer "Indiana" and got here at night, and we had supper for them and the house all lighted up. Well, you ought to have seen mother's old face! I'll never forget that night if I live to be a hundred. After that mother took in boarders and Joseph and Phil was there. We all put every cent we earned into building associations. So Tilly owned a house when she died and I own this one now. Our ladies told us how to put the money so as to breed more, and we never spent a cent we could save. Joseph pushed on and got big wages and started a flour store, and Phil went to night school and got a place as clerk. He married a teacher in the Kensington public school. She was a showy miss! Silk dress and feathers in her hat!

Joseph did well in his flour store. He has a big one on Market Street now and lives in a pretty house out in West

Philadelphia. He's one of the wardens in his church out there and his girls give teas and go to reading clubs.

But Phil is the one to go ahead! And his son, young Phil, is in politics and a member of councils.

It was Phil that coaxed me to give up work at Mrs. Carr's and to open my house for boarders here in Kensington. His wife didn't like to hear it said I was working in somebody's kitchen.

I heard that young Phil told some of his friends that he had a queer old aunt up in Kensington who played poor, but had a great store of money hoarded away. He shouldn't have told a story like that. But young folks will be young! I like the boy. He is certainly bringing the family into notice in the world. Last Sunday's paper had his picture and one of the young lady he is going to marry in New York. It called him the young millionaire McNabb. But I judge he's not that. He wanted to borrow the money I have laid by in the old bank at Walnut and Seventh the other day and said he'd double it in a week. No such work as that for me! But the boy certainly is a credit to the family!

Ah-nen-la-de-ni
A Mohawk Tribesman

Native Americans are among those minority group members who have suffered most from injustice in America. After benefiting from the generous help offered by the Indians, the first settlers and those who followed repaid their benefactors by taking their land. By the last quarter of the nineteenth century, the sentiment of most white settlers could be expressed in the words, "The only good Indian is a dead Indian."

Those Native Americans who survived the systematic program of physical and cultural genocide meted out to them were sometimes offered an opportunity to succeed *on white terms. This meant training at a white institution that demanded they surrender their traditional beliefs and way of life. Ah-nen-la-de-ni, whose name means Turning Crowd, was given this choice. His memoir provides a vivid glimpse of what it meant to walk between two worlds.*

I was born in Governeur Village, N.Y., in April, *1879*, during one of the periodical wanderings of my family. My father was a pure-blooded Indian of the Mohawk tribe of the Six Nations, and our home was in the St. Regis reservation in Franklin County, N.Y., but we were frequently away from that place because my father was an Indian medicine man, who made frequent journeys, taking his family with him and selling his pills and physics in various towns along the borderline between Canada and the United States.

My father was rather a striking figure. His hair was long and black, and he wore a long Prince Albert coat while in the winter quarters, and Indian costume, fringed and beaded, while in the tent. His medicines were put up in pill boxes and labeled bottles, and were the results of knowledge that had been handed down through many generations in our tribe.

My brother and I also wore long hair, and were strange enough in appearance to attract attention from the white people about us, but mother kept us away from them as much as possible.

My father was not only a doctor, but also a trapper, fisherman, farmer, and basket-maker.

The reservation in Franklin County is a very beautiful place, fronting on the main St. Lawrence River. On this reservation we had our permanent home in a log house surrounded by land, on which we planted corn, potatoes, and such other vegetables as suited our fancies. The house was more than fifty years old.

The woods provided my father and grandmother with their herbs and roots, and they gathered there the materials for basket-making. We were generally on the reservation in early spring, planting, fishing, basket-making, gathering herbs and making medicine, and then in the fall, when our little crop was brought in, we would depart on our tour of the white man's towns and cities, camping in a tent on the outskirts of some place, selling our wares, which included bead work that mother and grandmother were clever at making, and moving on as the fancy took us until cold weather came, when my father would generally build a little log house in some wood, plastering the chinks with moss and clay, and there we would abide, warm amid ice and snow, till it was time to go to the reservation again.

One might imagine that with such a great variety of occupations we would soon become rich—especially as we raised much of our own food and seldom had any rent to pay—but this was not the case. I do not know how much my father charged for his treatment of sick people, but his prices were probably moderate, and as to our trade in baskets, furs and bead work, we were not any better business people than Indians generally.

Nevertheless, it was a happy life that we led, and lack of money troubled us little. We were healthy and our wants were few.

Father did not always take his family with him on his expeditions, and as I grew older I passed a good deal of time on the reservation. Here, tho the people farmed and dressed somewhat after the fashion of the white man, they still kept up their ancient tribal ceremonies, laws, and customs, and preserved their language. The general government was in the hands of twelve chiefs, elected for life on account of supposed merit and ability.

There were four Indian day schools on the reservation, all taught by young white women. I sometimes went to one of these, but learned practically nothing. The teachers did not understand our language, and we knew nothing of theirs, so much progress was not possible.

Our lessons consisted of learning to repeat all the English words in the books that were given us. Thus, after a time, some of us, myself included, became able to pronounce all the words in the fifth and sixth readers, and took great pride in the exercise. But we did not know what any of the words meant.

Our arithmetic stopped at simple numeration, and the only other exercise we had was in writing, which, with us, resolved itself into a contest of speed without regard to the form of letters.

The Indian parents were disgusted with the schools, and did not urge their children to attend, and when the boys and girls did go of their own free will it was more for sociability and curiosity than from a desire to learn.

Ah-nen-la-de-ni, A Mohawk Tribesman

Many of the boys and girls were so large that the teachers could not preserve discipline, and we spent much of our time in the school drawing pictures of each other and the teacher, and exchanging in our own language such remarks as led to a great deal of fighting when we regained the open air. Often boys went home with their clothing torn off them in these fights.

Under the circumstances, it is not strange that the attendance at these schools was poor and irregular, and that on many days the teachers sat alone in the schoolhouses because there were no scholars. Since that time a great change has taken place, and there are now good schools on the reservation.

I was an official of one of the schools, to the extent that I chopped wood for it, but I did not often attend its sessions, and when I was thirteen years of age, and had been nominally a pupil of the school for six years, I was still so ignorant of English that I only knew one sentence, which was common property among us alleged pupils: "Please, ma'am, can I go out?" Pronounced: "Peezumgannigowout!"

When I was thirteen a great change occurred, for the honey-tongued agent of a new government-contract Indian school appeared on the reservation, drumming up boys and girls for his institution. He made a great impression by going from house to house and describing, through an interpreter, all the glories and luxuries of the new place, the good food and teaching, the fine uniforms, the playground and its sports and toys.

All that a wild Indian boy had to do, according to the

agent, was to attend this school for a year or two, and he was sure to emerge therefrom with all the knowledge and skill of the white man.

My father was away from the reservation at the time of the agent's arrival, but mother and grandmother heard him with growing wonder and interest, as I did myself, and we all finally decided that I ought to go to this wonderful school and become a great man—perhaps at last a chief of our tribe. Mother said that it was good for Indians to be educated, as white men were "so tricky with papers."

I had, up to this time, been leading a very happy life, helping with the planting, trapping, fishing, basket-making and playing all the games of my tribe—which is famous at lacrosse—but the desire to travel and see new things and the hope of finding an easy way to much knowledge in the wonderful school outweighed my regard for my home and its joys, and so I was one of the twelve boys who in 1892 left our reservation to go to the government-contract school for Indians, situated in a large Pennsylvania city and known as the ――― Institute.

Till I arrived at the school I had never heard that there were any other Indians in the country other than those of our reservation, and I did not know that our tribe was called Mohawk. My people called themselves "Ga-nien-ge-ha-ga," meaning "People of the Beacon Stone" and Indians generally they termed "On-give-hon-we," meaning "Real-men" or "Primitive People."

My surprise, therefore, was great when I found myself surrounded in the schoolyard by strange Indian boys belonging to tribes of which I had never heard, and when it was said that my people were only the "civilized Mohawks," I at first thought that "Mohawk" was a nickname and fought any boy who called me by it.

I had left home for the school with a great deal of hope, having said to my mother: "Do not worry. I shall soon return to you a better boy and with a good education!" Little did I dream that that was the last time I would ever see her kind face. She died two years later, and I was not allowed to go to her funeral.

The journey to Philadelphia had been very enjoyable and interesting. It was my first ride on the "great steel horse," as the Indians called the railway train, but my frame of mind changed as soon as my new home was reached.

The first thing that happened to me and to all other freshly caught young redskins when we arrived at the institution was a bath of a particularly disconcerting sort. We were used to baths of the swimming variety, for on the reservation we boys spent a good deal of our time in the water, but this first bath at the institution was different. For one thing, it was accompanied by plenty of soap, and for another thing, it was preceded by a haircut that is better described as a crop.

The little newcomer, thus cropped and delivered over to the untender mercies of larger Indian boys of tribes different from his own, who laughingly attacked his bare skin with very hot water and very hard scrubbing brushes, was likely to emerge from the encounter with a clean skin but perturbed mind. When, in addition, he was prevented from expressing his feelings in the only language he knew, what wonder if some rules of the school were broken.

After the astonishing bath the newcomer was freshly clothed from head to foot, while the raiment in which he came from the reservation was burned or buried. Thereafter he was released by the torturers, and could be seen sidling about the corridors like a lonely crab, silent, sulky, immaculately clean, and most disconsolate.

After my bath and reclothing and after having had my name taken down in the records, I was assigned to a dormitory, and began my regular school life, much to my dissatisfaction. The recording of my name was accompanied by a change which, though it might seem trifling to the teachers, was very important to me. My name among my own people was "Ah-nen-la-de-ni," which in English means "Turning Crowd" or "Turns the Crowd," but my family had had the name "La France" bestowed on them by the French some generations before my birth, and at the institution my Indian name was discarded, and I was informed that I was henceforth to be known as Daniel La France.

It made me feel as if I had lost myself. I had been proud of myself and my possibilities as "Turns the Crowd," for in spite of their civilized surroundings the Indians of our reservation in my time still looked back to the old warlike days when the Mohawks were great people, but Daniel La France was to me a stranger and a nobody with no possibilities. It seemed as if my prospect of a chiefship had vanished. I was very homesick for a long time.

The dormitory to which I was assigned had twenty beds in it and was under a captain, who was one of the advanced scholars. It was his duty to teach and enforce the rules of the place in this room, and to report to the white authorities all breaches of discipline.

Out in the schoolyard there was the same sort of supervision. Whether at work or play, we were constantly watched, and there were those in authority over us. This displeased us Mohawks, who were warriors at fourteen years of age.

After the almost complete freedom of reservation life the cramped quarters and the dull routine of the school were maddening to all us strangers. There were endless rules for us to study and abide by, and hardest of all was the rule against speaking to each other in our own language. We had to speak English or remain silent, and those who knew no English were forced to be dumb or else break the rules in secret. This last we did quite frequently and were punished when detected, by being made to stand in the "public hall" for a long time or to march about the yard while the other boys were at play.

There were about *115* boys at this school, and three miles from us was a similar government school for Indian girls, which had nearly as many inmates.

The system when I first went to this school contemplated every Indian boy learning a trade as well as getting a grammar school education. Accordingly we went to school in the morning and to work in the afternoon, or the other way about.

There were shoemakers, blacksmiths, tinsmiths, farmers, printers, all sorts of mechanics among us. I was set to learn the tailoring trade, and stuck at it for two and a half years, making such progress that I was about to be taught cutting when I began to cough, and it was said that outdoor work would be better for me. Accordingly I went, during the vacation of *1895,* up into Bucks County, Pa., and worked on a farm with benefit to my health, tho I was not a very successful farmer—the methods of the people who employed me were quite different from those of our reservation.

After I had finished with the grammar school I got a situation in the office of a lawyer while still residing in the institution. I also took a course of stenography and typewriting at the Philadelphia Young Men's Christian Association. So practically I was only a boarder at the institute during the latter part of my eight years' stay there.

Nevertheless, I was valuable to the authorities there for certain purposes, and when I wanted to leave and go to Carlisle School, which I had heard was very good, I could not obtain permission.

This institute, as I have said, was a government-contract school for teaching Indians. The great exertions made by the agent, who visited our reservation in the first place, were caused by the fact that a certain number of Indian children had to be obtained before the school could be opened. I do not think that the Indian parents signed any papers, but we boys and girls were supposed to remain at the school for five years. After that, as I understand it, we were free from any obligation.

The reason why I and others like me were kept at the

school was that we served as show scholars—as results of the system and evidences of the good work the institute was doing.

When I first went to the school the superintendent was a clergyman, honest and well meaning, and during the first five years thereafter while he remained in charge the general administration was honest, but when he went away the school entered upon a period of changing administrations and general demoralization. New superintendents succeeded each other at short intervals, and some of them were violent and cruel, while all seemed to us boys more or less dishonest. Boys who had been inmates of the school for eight years were shown to visitors as results of two years' tuition, and shoes and other articles bought in Philadelphia stores were hung up on the walls at public exhibition or concert and exhibited as the work of us boys. I was good for various show purposes. I could sing and play a musical instrument, and I wrote essays which were thought to be very good. The authorities also were fond of displaying me as one who had come to the school a few years before unable to speak a word of English.

Over the superintendent of the institute there was a Board of Lady Managers with a Lady Directress, and these visited us occasionally, but there was no use laying any complaint before them. They were arbitrary and almost unapproachable. Matters went from bad to worse, and when the Spanish-American War broke out, and my employer, the lawyer, resolved to go to it in the Red Cross service and offered to take me with him I greatly desired to go, but was not allowed. I suppose that the lawyer could easily have obtained my liberty, but did not wish to antagonize the Lady Managers, who considered any criticism of the institution as an attack on their own infallibility.

While waiting for a new situation after the young lawyer had gone away, I heard of the opportunities there were for young men who could become good nurses, and of the place where such training could be secured. I desired to go there and presented this ambition to the superintendent, who at first encouraged me to the extent of giving a fair recommendation. But when the matter was laid before the Head Directress in the shape of an application for admission ready to be sent by me to the authorities of the Nurses' Training School, she flatly refused it consideration without giving any good reason for doing so.

She, however, made the mistake of returning the application to me, and it was amended later and sent to the Training School in Manhattan. It went out through a secret channel, as all the regular mail of the institution's inmates, whether outgoing or incoming, was opened and examined in the office of the superintendent.

A few days before the 4th of July, *1899,* the answer to my application arrived in the form of notice to report at the school for the entrance examination. This communication found me in the school jail, where I had been placed for the first time in all my life at the institution.

I had been charged with throwing a nightgown out of the dormitory window, and truly it was my nightgown that was found in the schoolyard, for it had my number upon it. But I never threw it out of the window. I believe that one of the official underlings did that in order to found upon it a charge against me, for the school authorities had discovered that I and other boys of the institution had gone to members of the Indian Rights Association and had made complaint of conditions in the school, and that an investigation was coming. They, therefore, desired to disgrace and punish me as one of the leaders of those who were exposing them.

I heard about the letter from the Training School, and was very anxious to get away, but my liberation in time to attend that entrance examination seemed impossible. The days passed, and when the 4th of July arrived I was still in the school jail, which was the rear part of a stable.

At one o'clock my meal of bread and water was brought to me by the guard detailed to look after my safekeeping. After he had delivered this to me he went outside, leaving the door open, but standing there. The only window of that stable was very small, very high on the wall and was protected by iron bars—but here was the door left open.

I fled, and singularly enough the guard had his back turned and was contemplating nature with great assiduity. As soon as I got out of the enclosure I dashed after and caught a trolley car, and a few hours later I was in New York.

That was the last I saw of the institute and it soon afterward went out of existence, but I heard that as a result of the demand for an investigation the Superintendent of Indian Schools had descended on it upon a given day and found everything beautiful—for her visit had been announced. But she returned again the next day, when it was supposed that she had left the city, and then things were not beautiful at all, and much that we had told about was proven.

An Anonymous Coal Miner

In 1902 the United Mine Workers in the anthracite region of Pennsylvania called a strike for higher pay and union recognition and 15,000 miners walked out of the coal pits. Mine owners responded by calling in strikebreakers and soon there were shootings, bombings, and riots. As the cold weather approached, the UMW proposed arbitration.

The coal operators rejected it. President George F. Baer of the Reading Railroad voiced their private views when he declared: "The rights and interests of the laboring man will be protected and cared for—not by labor agitators, but by the Christian men to whom God in His infinite wisdom has given the control of the property interests of the country."

George F. Baer's words reveal the attitudes of one side—the side of the wealthy and privileged. But the words of the anonymous coal miner who participated in this strike form a fascinating contrast and deserve an equal place in the historical record.

I am thirty-five years old, married, the father of four children, and have lived in the coal region all my life. Twenty-three of these years have been spent working in and around the mines. My father was a miner. He died ten years ago from "miners' asthma."

Three of my brothers are miners; none of us had any opportunities to acquire an education. We were sent to school (such a school as there was in those days) until we were about twelve years of age, and then we were put into the screen room of a breaker to pick slate. From there we went inside the mines as driver boys. As we grew stronger we were taken on as laborers, where we served until able to call ourselves miners. We were given work in the breasts and gangways. There were five of us boys. One lies in the cemetery—fifty tons of top rock dropped on him. He was killed three weeks after he got his job as a miner—a month before he was to be married.

In the fifteen years I have worked as a miner I have earned the average rate of wages any of us coal heavers get. Today I am little better off than when I started to do for myself. I have *$100* on hand; I am not in debt; I hope to be able to weather the strike without going hungry.

I am only one of the hundreds you see on the street every day. The muscles on my arms are no harder, the callous on my palms no deeper than my neighbor's whose entire life has been spent in the coal region. By years I am only thirty-five. But look at the marks on my body; look at the lines of worriment on my forehead; see the gray hairs on my head and in my mustache; take my general appearance, and you'll think I'm ten years older.

You need not wonder why. Day in and day out, from Monday morning to Saturday evening, between the rising and the setting of the sun, I am in the underground workings of the coal mines. From the seams water trickles into the ditches along the gangways; if not water, it is the gas which hurls us to eternity and the props and timbers to a chaos.

Our daily life is not a pleasant one. When we put on our oil soaked suit in the morning we can't guess all the dangers which threaten our lives. We walk sometimes miles to the place—to the man way or traveling way, or to the mouth of the shaft on top of the slope. And then we enter the darkened chambers of the mines. On our right and on our left we see the logs that keep up the top and support the sides which may crush us into shapeless masses, as they have done to many of our comrades.

We get old quickly. Powder, smoke, after-damp, bad air—all combine to bring furrows to our faces and asthma to our lungs.

I did not strike because I wanted to; I struck because I had to. A miner—the same as any other workman—must earn fair living wages, or he can't live. And it is not how much you get that counts. It is how much what you get will buy. I have gone through it all, and I think my case is a good sample.

I was married in *1890,* when I was twenty-three years old—quite a bit above the age when we miner boys get into double harness. The woman I married is like myself. She was born beneath the shadow of a dirt bank; her chances for school weren't any better than mine; but she did have to learn how to keep house on a certain amount of money. After we paid the preacher for tying the knot we had just *$185* in cash, good health, and the good wishes of many friends to start us off.

Our cash was exhausted in buying furniture for housekeeping. In *1890* work was not so plentiful, and by the time our first baby came there was room for much doubt as to how we would pull out. Low wages, and not much over half time in those years, made us hustle. In *1890–91,* from June to May *1,* I earned *$368.72.* That represented eleven months' work, or an average of *$33.52* per month. Our rent was *$10* per month; store not less than *$20*. And then I had my oil suits and gum boots to pay for. The result was that after the first year and a half of our married life we were in debt. Not much, of course, and not as much as many of my neighbors, men of larger families, and some who made less money, or in whose case there had been sickness or accident or death. These are all things which a miner must provide for.

An Anonymous Coal Miner

In *1896* my wife was sick eleven weeks. The doctor came to my house almost every day. He charged me $20 for his services. There was medicine to buy. I paid the drugstore $18 in that time. Her mother nursed her, and we kept a girl in the kitchen at $1.50 a week, which cost me $15 for ten weeks, besides the additional living expenses.

In *1897,* just a year afterward, I had a severer trial. And mind, in those years, we were only working about half time. But in the fall of that year one of my brothers struck a gas feeder. There was a terrible explosion. He was hurled downward in the breast and covered with the rush of coal and rock. I was working only three breasts away from him and for a moment was unable to realize what had occurred. Myself and a hundred others were soon at work, however, and in a short while we found him, horribly burned over his whole body, his laborer dead alongside of him.

He was my brother. He was single and had been boarding. He had no home of his own. I didn't want him taken to the hospital, so I directed the driver of the ambulance to take him to my house. Besides being burned, his right arm and left leg were broken, and he was hurt internally. The doctors—there were two at the house when we got there—said he would die. But he didn't. He is living and a miner today. But he lay in bed just fourteen weeks, and was unable to work for seven weeks after he got out of bed. He had no money when he was hurt except the amount represented by his pay. All of the expenses for doctors, medicine, extra help, and his living were borne by me, except $25, which another brother gave me. The last one had none to give. Poor work, low wages, and a sickly woman for a wife had kept him scratching for his own family.

It is nonsense to say I was not compelled to keep him, that I could have sent him to a hospital or the almshouse. We are American citizens and we don't go to hospitals and poorhouses.

Let us look at things as they are today, or as they were before the strike commenced.

My last pay envelope shows my wages, after my laborer, powder, oil, and other expenses were taken off, were *$29.47;* that was my earning for two weeks, and that was extra good. The laborer for the same time got some *$21*. His wages are a trifle over *$10* a week for six full days. Before the strike of *1900* he was paid in this region *$1.70* per day, or *$10.20* a week. If the ten percent raise had been given, as we expected, his wages would be *$1.87* per day, or *$11.22* per week, or an increase of *$1.02* per week. But we all know that under the present system he doesn't get any eleven dollars.

Well, as I said my wages were *$29.47* for the two weeks, or at the rate of *$58.94* per month. My rent is *$10.50* per month. My coal costs me almost *$4* per month. We burn a little over a ton a month on an average and it costs us over *$3* per ton. Light does not cost so much; we use coal oil altogether.

When it comes down to groceries is where you get hit the hardest. Everybody knows the cost of living has been extremely high all winter. Butter has been *32, 36,* and *38* cents a pound; eggs as high as *32* cents a dozen; ham, *12* and *16* cents a pound; potatoes away up to a dollar, and cabbage not less than a cent a pound. Fresh meat need not be counted. Flour and sugar did not advance, but they were about the only staples that didn't. Anyhow, my store bill for those two weeks was *$11*. That makes *$22* per month. The butcher gets *$6* per month. Add them all, and it costs me, just to live, *$42.50*. That leaves me *$17* per month to keep my family in clothes, to pay my church dues and to keep the industrial insurance going. My insurance alone costs me *55* cents a week, or *$2.20* a month.

The coal president never allows his stable boss to cut the amount of fodder allotted to his mules. He insists on so many quarts of oats and corn to the meal and so much hay in the evening. The mule must be fed; the miner may be, if he works hard enough and earns money to buy the grub.

Company stores are of the time that has been. Their existence ended two years ago. But we've got a system growing up that threatens to be just as bad. Let me explain. Over a year ago I was given a breast to drive at one of our mines and was glad to get it. My wife took her cash and went around the different places to buy. When I went to the office for my first pay the "super" met me and asked me if I didn't know his wife's brother George kept a store. I answered, "Yes," and wanted to know what that had to do with it.

"Nothing, only I thought I'd call your attention to it," he answered.

No more was said then. But the next day I got a quiet tip that my breast was to be abandoned. This set me thinking. I went to the boss and, after a few words, told him my wife had found brother-in-law George's store and that she liked it much better than where she had bought before. I told him the other store didn't sell the right kind of silk waists, and their patent-leather shoes were away back. Brother-in-law George had the right kind of stuff and, of course, we were willing to pay a few cents more to get just what we wanted.

That was sarcastic, but it's the cash that has the influence. I have had work at that colliery ever since. I know my living costs me from 10 to 15 percent extra. But I kept my job, which meant a good deal.

Now you must take into consideration that I am a contract miner and that my earnings are more than the wages of three-fourths of the other fellows at the same colliery. It is not that I am a favorite with the boss. I just struck a good breast. Maybe next month my wages would be from two to six or seven dollars less.

In the days of Pardee, Coxe, Fagley, Fulton, Dewees, Paterson, Riley, Repplier, Graeber, and a hundred others, men were better paid than they have ever been since the centralization ideas of the late Franklin B. Gowen became fixed institutions in the anthracite counties. It may be true that in the days of the individual operation the cost per ton of mining coal was less than it is today. But it is not right that the entire increase in the cost of mining be charged to the miner. That is what is being done, if you count the reductions made in wages.

We miners do not participate in the high prices of coal. The operators try to prove otherwise by juggling with figures, but their proving has struck a fault, and

An Anonymous Coal Miner

the drill shows no coal in that section. One-half of the price paid for a ton of coal in New York or Philadelphia goes into the profit pocket of the mine owner, either as a carrier or miner.

We all know that the price of coal has advanced in the past twenty years. We also know that wages are less, that the cost of living is higher. I remember the time, when I was a wee lad, my father used to get his coal for *$1* per ton. Now I pay *$3*. In those days we lads used to go to the dirt banks and pick a load of coal, and it cost our parents only a half a dollar to get it hauled home. We dare not do that now. Then we did not need gum boots, safety lamps or any such things as that; and for all of them we must now pay out of wages that have been reduced.

Our condition can be no worse; it might and must be better. The luxuries of the rich we do not ask; we do want butter for our bread and meat for our soup. We do not want silk and laces for our wives and daughters. But we want to earn enough to buy them a clean calico once in a while. Our boys are not expecting automobiles and membership cards in clubs of every city, but they want their fathers to earn enough to keep them at school until they have a reasonably fair education.

Nat Love
Cowboy

~~~

Nat Love, known as Deadwood Dick, was born in a Tennessee slave cabin before the Civil War. He was one of thousands of Black, white, and Chicano cowpunchers who drove cattle up the Chisholm Trail. With obvious relish and swaggering self-assurance, Love fought outlaws, Indians, and lawmen; braved hailstones, swollen rivers, and rampaging cattle herds; battled wild animals; and lived to tell his tale in typical western braggadocio.

Actually, most cowpunchers of the last century had a terribly dull, sometimes hazardous, and always low-paying job. Excessive boasting and gunplay became the

Nat Love, Cowboy

means of reconciling a hearty, swashbuckling personality with tedious work and long, lonely nights on the western prairies.

The tall tales related by men like Nat Love helped create the enduring myth of the cowboy, the great American hero.

In an old log cabin, on my Master's plantation in Davidson County in Tennessee in June, *1854,* I first saw the light of day. The exact date of my birth I never knew, because in those days no count was kept of such trivial matters as the birth of a slave baby. . . .

It was on the tenth day of February, *1869,* that I left the old home near Nashville, Tennessee. I was at that time about fifteen years old, and though while young in years the hard work and farm life had made me strong and hearty, much beyond my years, and I had full confidence in myself as being able to take care of myself and make my way.

I at once struck out for Kansas of which I had heard something. And believing it was a good place in which to seek employment. It was in the West, and it was the great West I wanted to see, and so by walking and occasional lifts from farmers going my way and taking advantage of everything that promised to assist me on my way, I eventually brought up at Dodge City, Kansas, which at that time was a typical frontier city, with a great many saloons, dance halls, and gambling houses, and very little of anything else.

MAKING OUR WAY

When I arrived the town was full of cowboys from the surrounding ranches, and from Texas and other parts of the West. As Kansas was a great cattle center and market, the wild cowboy, prancing horses of which I was very fond, and the wild life generally, all had their attractions for me, and I decided to try for a place with them. . . .

During the big round-ups it was our duty to pick out our brand, and then send them home under the charge of our cowboys, likewise the newly branded stock. After each brand was cut out and started homeward, we had to stay with the round-up to see that strays from the different herds from the surrounding country did not again get mixed up, until the different home ranges were reached. This work employed a large number of cowboys, who lived, ate, and often slept in the saddle, as they covered many hundreds of miles in a very short space of time. This was made possible as every large cattleman had relays of horses sent out over the country where we might be expected to touch, and so we could always count on finding a fresh horse awaiting us at the end of a twenty-five or a fifty-mile ride. But for us brand readers there was no rest; we merely changed our saddles and outfit to a fresh horse and were again on the go. After the general round-up was over, cowboy sports and a good time generally was in order for those engaged in it.

In order to get the cattle together in the first general round-up, we would have to ride for hundreds of miles over the country in search of the long-horn steers and old cows that had drifted from the home range during the winter and were now scattered to the four winds of heaven. As soon as they were found they were started off under the care of cowboys for the place agreed upon for the general round-up, whether they belonged to us or not, while the rest of us continued the search. All the cowboys from the many different outfits working this way enabled us to soon get all the strays rounded up in one great herd in which the cattle of a dozen different owners were mixed up together. It then became our duty to cut out our different herds and start them homewards. Then we had to brand the young stock that had escaped that ordeal at the hands of the range riders. On finding the strays and starting them homewards, we had to keep up the search, because notwithstanding the fact that we had done range riding or line riding all winter, a large number of cattle would manage to evade the vigilance of the cowboys and get away. These must all be accounted for at the great round-up, as they stood for dollars and cents, profit and loss to the great cattle kings of the West.

In going after these strayed and perhaps stolen cattle we boys always provided ourselves with everything we needed, including plenty of grub, as sometimes we would be gone for nearly two months and sometimes much longer. It was not an uncommon occurrence for us to have shooting trouble over our different brands. In such disputes the boys would kill each other if others did not interfere in time to prevent it, because in those days on the great cattle ranges there was no law but the law of might, and all disputes were settled with a forty-five Colt pistol. In such cases the man who was quickest on the draw and whose eye was the best, pretty generally got the decision. Therefore it was of the greatest importance that the cowboy should understand his gun, its capabilities, and its shooting qualities. A cowboy would never carry anything but the very best gun obtainable, as his life depended on it often. After securing a good gun the cowboy had to learn how to use it, if he did not already know how. In doing so no trouble or expense was spared, and I know there were very few poor shots on the ranges over which we rode and they used the accomplishment to protect themselves and their employer's cattle from the Indian thieves and the white desperadoes who infested the cattle country, and who lost no opportunity to stampede the herds and run off large numbers of them. Whenever this happened it generally resulted in a long chase and a fierce fight in which someone was sure to get hurt, and hurt badly. But that fact did not bother us in the least. It was all simply our duty and our business for which we were paid and paid good, and so we accepted things as they came, always ready for it whatever it might be, and always taking pride in our work in which we always tried to excel.

We arrived in Deadwood in good condition without having had any trouble with the Indians on the way up. We turned our cattle over to their new owners at once, then proceeded to take in the town. The next morning, July 4th, the gamblers and mining men made up a purse of $200 for a roping contest between the cowboys that were then in town, and as it was a holiday nearly all the cowboys for miles around were assembled there that

Workers leaving a Massachusetts shoe factory

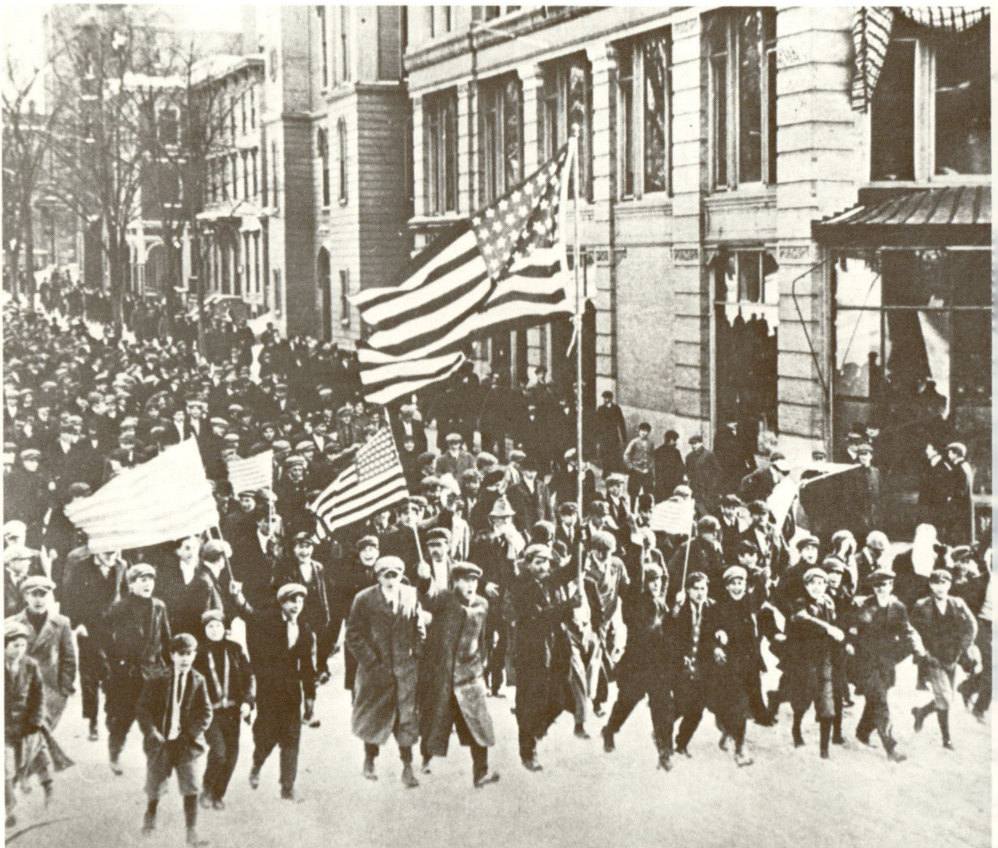

*Strikes and marches were workers' only
defense against exploitation.*

A Black sharecropper family in the South

Black cowboy Nat Love

Pennsylvania coal miners

The feast of St. Rocco on New York's Mulberry Street

San Francisco's Chinatown

An Italian immigrant boy learns to write.

day. It did not take long to arrange the details for the contest and contestants, six of them being colored cowboys, including myself. Our trail boss was chosen to pick out the mustangs from a herd of wild horses just off the range, and he picked out twelve of the most wild and vicious horses that he could find.

The conditions of the contest were that each of us who were mounted was to rope, throw, tie, bridle and saddle, and mount the particular horse picked for us in the shortest time possible. The man accomplishing the feat in the quickest time was to be declared the winner.

It seems to me that the horse chosen for me was the most vicious of the lot. Everything being in readiness, the *"45"* cracked and we all sprang forward together, each of us making for our particular mustang.

I roped, threw, tied, bridled, saddled, and mounted my mustang in exactly nine minutes from the crack of the gun. The time of the next nearest competitor was twelve minutes and thirty seconds. This gave me the record and championship of the West, which I held up to the time I quit the business in *1890*, and my record has never been beaten. It is worthy of passing remark that I never had a horse pitch with me so much as that mustang, but I never stopped sticking my spurs in him and using my quirt on his flanks until I proved his master. Right there the assembled crowd named me Deadwood Dick and proclaimed me champion roper of the western cattle country.

The roping contest over, a dispute arose over the shooting question with the result that a contest was arranged for the afternoon, as there happened to be some of the best shots with rifle and revolver in the West present that day. Among them were Stormy Jim, who claimed the championship; Powder Horn Bill, who had the reputation of never missing what he shot at; also White Head, a half-breed, who generally hit what he shot at, and many other men who knew how to handle a rifle or *45* Colt.

The range was measured off *100* and *250* yards for the rifle and *150* for the Colt *45*. At this distance a bull's-eye about the size of an apple was put up. Each man was to have *14* shots at each range with the rifle and *12* shots with the Colt *45*. I placed every one of my *14* shots with the rifle in the bull's-eye with ease, all shots being made from the hip; but with the *45* Colt I missed it twice, only placing *10* shots in the small circle, Stormy Jim being my nearest competitor, only placing *8* bullets in the bull's-eye clear, and the rest being quite close, while with the *45* he placed *5* bullets in the charmed circle. This gave me the championship of rifle and revolver shooting as well as the roping contest, and for that day I was the hero of Deadwood, and the purse of *$200* which I had won on the roping contest went toward keeping things moving, and they did move as only a large crowd of cattle men can move things. This lasted for several days when most of the cattle men had to return to their respective ranches, as it was the busy season; accordingly our outfit began to make preparations to return to Arizona.

§ *112* §

Lee Chew
Chinese American

From the time the Chinese began to come to America in large numbers during the California Gold Rush in 1849, they were viewed with suspicion and treated with hostility. The majority of those who came were single males. Many originally intended to stay only until they made enough money to return home with some savings, and they did not surrender their own culture for that which they found in the United States.

Their readiness to work hard for low pay—first demonstrated on the transcontinental railroad during the Civil War—made them the targets of white workingmen who resented them as job competitors. In 1883, Chinese were denied entrance to the United States. By the close of the nineteenth century, the Chinese had been shunned by labor unions, confined in ghettos, and attacked by mobs. They survived, however, because of strong family ties and a proud cultural tradition that viewed hostility from the outside as proof of their own superiority.

Most Chinese in America, unlike Lee Chew, were not successful storekeepers but menials, day laborers, and workers in the Chinese ghetto. Chew's castigation of Americans under his own signature represents no little courage for the Chinese American of his day. His attack on other immigrant groups was typical of those who faced persecution in America and suspected that others had it easier.

The village where I was born is situated in the province of Canton, on one of the banks of the Si-Kiang River. All in the village belonged to the tribe of Lee. They did not intermarry with one another, but the men went to other villages for their wives and brought them home to their fathers' houses, and men from other villages—Wus and Wings and Sings and Fongs, etc.—chose wives from among our girls.

When I was a baby I was kept in our house all the time with my mother, but when I was a boy of seven I had to sleep at nights with other boys of the village— about thirty of them in one house. The girls are separated the same way—thirty or forty of them sleeping together

Lee Chew, Chinese American

in one house away from their parents—and the widows have houses where they work and sleep, tho they go to their fathers' houses to eat.

In spite of the fact that any man may correct them for a fault, Chinese boys have good times and plenty of play. We played games like tag, and other games like shinny and a sort of football called yin.

It was not all play for us boys, however. We had to go to school, where we learned to read and write and to recite the precepts of Kong-foo-tsze and the other Sages, and stories about the great emperors of China, who ruled with the wisdom of gods and gave to the whole world the light of high civilization and the culture of our literature, which is the admiration of all nations.

I went to my parents' house for meals, approaching my grandfather with awe, my father and mother with veneration, and my elder brother with respect. I worked on my father's farm till I was about sixteen years of age, when a man of our tribe came back from America and took ground as large as four city blocks and made a paradise of it. He put a large stone wall around and led some streams through and built a palace and summer house and about twenty other structures, with beautiful bridges over the streams and walks and roads. Trees and flowers, singing birds, waterfowl, and curious animals were within his walls.

The man had gone away from our village a poor boy. Now he returned with unlimited wealth, which he had obtained in the country of the American wizards. After many amazing adventures he had become a merchant in a city called Mott Street, so it was said.

The wealth of this man filled my mind with the idea that I, too, would like to go to the country of the wizards and gain some of their wealth, and after a long time my father consented, and gave me his blessing, and my mother took leave of me with tears, while my grandfather laid his hand upon my head and told me to remember and live up to the admonitions of the Sages, to avoid gambling, bad women, and men of evil minds, and so to govern my conduct that when I died my ancestors might rejoice to welcome me as a guest on high.

My father gave me *$100,* and I went to Hong Kong with five other boys from our place and we got steerage passage on a steamer, paying *$50* each. Everything was new to me. All my life I had been used to sleeping on a board bed with a wooden pillow, and I found the steamer's bunk very uncomfortable, because it was so soft. The food was different from that which I had been used to, and I did not like it at all. I was afraid of the stews, for the thought of what they might be made of by the wicked wizards of the ship made me ill. When I got to San Francisco, which was before the passage of the Exclusion Act, I was half starved, because I was afraid to eat the provisions of the barbarians, but a few days' living in the Chinese quarter made me happy again. A man got me work as a house servant in an American family, and my start was the same as that of almost all the Chinese in this country.

The Chinese laundryman does not learn his trade in China; there are no laundries in China. The women there do the washing in tubs and have no washboards or flat

Lee Chew, Chinese American

irons. All the Chinese laundrymen here were taught in the first place by American women just as I was taught.

When I went to work for that American family I could not speak a word of English, and I did not know anything about housework. The family consisted of husband, wife, and two children. They were very good to me and paid me $3.50 a week, of which I could save $3.

I did not know how to do anything, and I did not understand what the lady said to me, but she showed me how to cook, wash, iron, sweep, dust, make beds, wash dishes, clean windows, paint and brass, polish the knives and forks, etc., by doing the things herself and then overseeing my efforts to imitate her. She would take my hands and show them how to do things. She and her husband and children laughed at me a great deal, but it was all good natured. I was not confined to the house in the way servants are confined here, but when my work was done in the morning I was allowed to go out till lunchtime. People in California are more generous than they are here.

In six months I had learned how to do the work of our house quite well, and I was getting $5 a week and board, and putting away about $4.25 a week. I had also learned some English, and by going to a Sunday school I learned more English and something about Jesus, who was a great Sage, and whose precepts are like those of Kong-foo-tsze.

It was twenty years ago when I came to this country, and I worked for two years as a servant, getting at the last $35 a month. I sent money home to comfort my parents, but tho I dressed well and lived well and had pleasure, going quite often to the Chinese theater and to dinner parties in Chinatown, I saved *$50* in the first six months, *$90* in the second, *$120* in the third, and *$150* in the fourth. So I had *$410* at the end of two years, and I was now ready to start in business.

When I first opened a laundry it was in company with a partner, who had been in the business for some years. We went to a town about *500* miles inland, where a railroad was building. We got a board shanty and worked for the men employed by the railroads. Our rent cost was *$10* a month and food nearly *$5* a week each, for all food was dear and we wanted the best of everything— we lived principally on rice, chickens, ducks, and pork, and did our own cooking. The Chinese take naturally to cooking. It cost us about *$50* for our furniture and apparatus, and we made close upon *$60* a week, which we divided between us. We had to put up with many insults and some frauds, as men would come in and claim parcels that did not belong to them, saying they had lost their tickets, and would fight if they did not get what they asked for. Sometimes we were taken before magistrates and fined for losing shirts that we had never seen. On the other hand, we were making money, and even after sending home *$3* a week I was able to save about *$15*. When the railroad construction gang moved on we went with them. The men were rough and prejudiced against us, but not more so than in the big eastern cities. It is only lately in New York that the Chinese have been able to discontinue putting wire screens in front of their windows, and at the present time the streetboys are still breaking the windows of Chinese laundries all over the city, while the police seem to think it a joke.

We were three years with the railroad, and then went to the mines, where we made plenty of money in gold dust, but had a hard time, for many of the miners were wild men who carried revolvers and after drinking would come into our place to shoot and steal shirts, for which we had to pay. One of these men hit his head hard against a flat iron and all the miners came and broke up our laundry, chasing us out of town. They were going to hang us. We lost all our property and *$365* in money, which members of the mob must have found.

Luckily most of our money was in the hands of Chinese bankers in San Francisco. I drew *$500* and went east to Chicago, where I had a laundry for three years, during which I increased my capital to *$2,500*. After that I was four years in Detroit. I went home to China in *1897*, but returned in *1898* and began a laundry business in Buffalo. But Chinese laundry business now is not as good as it was ten years ago. American cheap labor in the steam laundries has hurt it. So I determined to become a general merchant, and with this idea I came to New York and opened a shop in the Chinese quarter, keeping silks, teas, porcelain, clothes, shoes, hats, and Chinese provisions, which include shark's fins and nuts, lily bulbs and lily flowers, lychee nuts, and other Chinese dainties, but do not include rats, because it would be too expensive to import them. The rat which is eaten by the Chinese is a field animal which lives on rice, grain, and sugar cane. Its flesh is delicious. Many Americans who have tasted shark's fin and bird's nest soup and tiger lily flowers and bulbs are firm friends of Chinese cookery. If they could enjoy one of our fine rats they would go to China to live, so as to get some more.

American people eat groundhogs, which are very like these Chinese rats, and they also eat many sorts of food that our people would not touch. Those that have dined with us know that we understand how to live well.

The ordinary laundry shop is generally divided into three rooms. In front is the room where the customers are received, behind that a bedroom and in the back the workshop, which is also the dining room and kitchen. The stove and cooking utensils are the same as those of the Americans.

Work in a laundry begins early on Monday morning—about seven o'clock. There are generally two men, one of whom washes while the other does the ironing. The man who irons does not start in till Tuesday, as the clothes are not ready for him to begin till that time. So he has Sundays and Mondays as holidays. The man who does the washing finishes up on Friday night, and so he has Saturday and Sunday. Each works only five days a week, but those are long days—from seven o'clock in the morning till midnight.

During his holidays the Chinaman gets a good deal of fun out of life. There's a good deal of gambling and some opium smoking, but not so much as Americans imagine. Only a few of New York's Chinamen smoke opium. The habit is very general among rich men and officials in China, but not so much among poor men. I don't think it does as much harm as the liquor that the Americans drink. There's nothing so bad as a drunken

Lee Chew, Chinese American

man. Opium doesn't make people crazy.

Gambling is mostly fan-tan, but there is a good deal of poker, which the Chinese have learned from Americans and can play very well. They also gamble with dominoes and dice.

The fights among the Chinese and the operations of the hatchet men are all due to gambling. Newspapers often say that they are feuds between the six companies, but that is a mistake. The six companies are purely benevolent societies, which look after the Chinaman when he first lands here. They represent the six southern provinces of China, where most of our people are from, and they are like the German, Swedish, English, Irish, and Italian societies which assist emigrants. When the Chinese keep clear of gambling and opium they are not blackmailed, and they have no trouble with hatchet men or any others.

About *500* of New York's Chinese are Christians, the others are Buddhists, Taoists, etc., all mixed up. These haven't any Sunday of their own, but keep New Year's Day and the first and fifteenth days of each month, when they go to the temple in Mott Street.

In all New York there are only thirty-four Chinese women, and it is impossible to get a Chinese woman out here unless one goes to China and marries her there, and then he must collect affidavits to prove that she really is his wife. That is in the case of a merchant. A laundryman can't bring his wife here under any circumstances, and even the women of the Chinese Ambassador's family had trouble getting in lately.

Is it any wonder, therefore, or any proof of the demoralization of our people if some of the white women in Chinatown are not of good character? What other set of men so isolated and so surrounded by alien and prejudiced people are more moral? Men, wherever they may be, need the society of women, and among the white women of Chinatown are many excellent and faithful wives and mothers.

Recently there has been organized among us the Oriental Club, composed of our most intelligent and influential men. We hope for a great improvement in social conditions by its means, as it will discuss matters that concern us, bring us in closer touch with Americans, and speak for us in something like an official manner.

Some fault is found with us for sticking to our old customs here, especially in the matter of clothes, but the reason is that we find American clothes much inferior, so far as comfort and warmth go. The Chinaman's coat for the winter is very durable, very light, and very warm. It is easy and not in the way. If he wants to work he slips out of it in a moment and can put it on again as quickly. Our shoes and hats also are better, we think, for our purposes, than the American clothes. Most of us have tried the American clothes, and they make us feel as if we were in the stocks.

I have found out, during my residence in this country, that much of the Chinese prejudice against Americans is unfounded, and I no longer put faith in the wild tales that were told about them in our village, tho some of the Chinese, who have been here twenty years and who are learned men, still believe that there is no marriage in this country, that the land is infested with demons, and

Lee Chew, Chinese American

that all the people are given over to general wickedness.

I know better. Americans are not all bad, nor are they wicked wizards. Still, they have their faults, and their treatment of us is outrageous.

The reason why so many Chinese go into the laundry business in this country is because it requires little capital and is one of the few opportunities that are open. Men of other nationalities who are jealous of the Chinese, because he is a more faithful worker than one of their people, have raised such a great outcry about Chinese cheap labor that they have shut him out of working on farms or in factories or building railroads or making streets or digging sewers. He cannot practice any trade, and his opportunities to do business are limited to his own countrymen. So he opens a laundry when he quits domestic service.

The treatment of the Chinese in this country is all wrong and mean. It is persisted in merely because China is not a fighting nation. The Americans would not dare to treat Germans, English, Italians, or even Japanese as they treat the Chinese, because if they did there would be a war.

There is no reason for the prejudice against the Chinese. The cheap labor cry was always a falsehood. Their labor was never cheap, and is not cheap now. It has always commanded the highest market price. But the trouble is that the Chinese are such excellent and faithful workers that bosses will have no others when they can get them. If you look at men working on the street you will find an overseer for every four or five of them. That watching is not necessary for Chinese. They work as well when left to themselves as they do when someone is looking at them.

It was the jealousy of laboring men of other nationalities—especially the Irish—that raised all the outcry against the Chinese. No one would hire an Irishman, German, Englishman, or Italian when he could get a Chinese, because our countrymen are so much more honest, industrious, steady, sober, and painstaking. Chinese were persecuted, not for their vices, but for their virtues. There never was any honesty in the pretended fear of leprosy or in the cheap labor scare, and the persecution continues still, because Americans make a mere practice of loving justice. They are all for money-making, and they want to be on the strongest side always. They treat you as a friend while you are prosperous, but if you have a misfortune they don't know you. There is nothing substantial in their friendship.

Wu-Ting-Fang talked very plainly to Americans about their ill treatment of our countrymen, but we don't see any good results. We hoped for good from Roosevelt, we thought him a brave and good man, but yet he has continued the exclusion of our countrymen, though all other nations are allowed to pour in here—Irish, Italians, Jews, Poles, Greeks, Hungarians, etc. It would not have been so if Mr. McKinley had lived.

Irish fill the almshouses and prisons and orphan asylums; Italians are among the most dangerous of men; Jews are unclean and ignorant. Yet they are all let in, while Chinese, who are sober, or duly law abiding, clean, educated, and industrious, are shut out. There are few Chinamen in jails and none in the poor houses. There are no Chinese tramps or drunkards. Many Chinese here have become sincere Christians, in spite of the persecution which they have to endure from their heathen countrymen. More than half the Chinese in this country would become citizens if allowed to do so, and would be patriotic Americans. But how can they make this country their home as matters now are! They are not allowed to bring wives here from China, and if they marry American women there is a great outcry.

All Congressmen acknowledge the injustice of the treatment of my people, yet they continue it. They have no backbone.

Under the circumstances, how can I call this my home, and how can any one blame me if I take my money and go back to my village in China?

An Anonymous Collar Starcher

Although women were five million strong in the labor force by 1900, trade unions shunned them almost as much as they shunned racial and ethnic minorities. Women's permanent place was in the home, it was said, and their loyalty to jobs and unions could only be temporary. As a result, women felt little personal investment in their jobs, in unions or strikes, except when other alternatives failed. Women were told it was unladylike to join a union, particularly since unions were run by "labor agitators" and foreigners committed to socialism or anarchism. Just as men believed in the American dream and hoped that

An Anonymous Collar Starcher

hard work or ingenious invention would release them from grueling labor, most women dreamed that marriage and motherhood would do the same for them.

But as the nineteenth century gave way to the twentieth, the unreality of such dreams became more and more evident. Disillusioned, women joined unions and struck for higher wages, better working conditions, and union recognition. They began to play a key part in labor disputes, providing the industrial scene with some of its most dramatically vivid moments. Fearing her recent part in a laundry workers' strike in Troy, New York, would result in her being blacklisted in the industry, this collar starcher dictated her memoir to a sympathetic female reporter but she stipulated that her name be withheld.

When I left school at the age of sixteen to go to work there were very few opportunities open to young girls, for the time was nearly thirty years ago. Therefore I considered myself unusually lucky to have been born and brought up in Troy, N.Y., where the shirt and collar factories offered employment to women. I was lucky also in being a large, stout girl, for the work offered me when I applied was that of a collar starcher, and while this does not call for much muscle, it certainly requires endurance and a good constitution. In those days practically all the laundry work was done by hand. There were no ironing machines and very few washing machines. The starching was about all there was for a girl of sixteen. So a starcher

I became and a starcher I am to this day, or rather, I was until the strike came in May.

I thoroughly enjoyed my first working years. The factory was not at all a bad place. I worked side by side with my friends, the girls I had gone to school with, met at church and at dances and picnics. The starching rooms were very hot and stuffy generally, like a Turkish bath, and the work was hard on the hands; but I didn't mind these discomforts. Looking back at it now I think we were very well off. There was nothing like the rush and hurry we live in now. We were not driven at such a furious pace, for, of course, there was not nearly the business done then that there is now.

The starching itself was a very different affair. The collars were two-ply, instead of the thick, unwieldy things men wear now, and there was no "lady work," as we say. We simply rubbed in heavy starch, using our hands and soft cloths. It was hot enough, but not the scalding work it is now.

The working hours were not too long—about eight hours a day. We went to work at nine o'clock, except in the busy season, when we were on hand at eight. The day passed quickly with the talk and sometimes a bit of song to liven things up. We used to sing part-songs and old-fashioned choruses. Some of the girls had beautiful voices.

We have to be at the tables at seven now and an ambitious worker is usually in the factory half an hour before the whistle blows, to get her table ready. As for talk or singing, the foreman would have a fit if anything like that should happen. In our factory all talking is strictly for-

An Anonymous Collar Starcher

bidden. You run the risk of instant dismissal if you even speak to the girl across the table. Even at the noon hour you can only whisper. I've seen girls discharged for talking and I know of a case where a girl lost her job for sneezing. The foreman said she did it on purpose. They are not as hard as this in all the factories. Much depends on the foreman.

My father and mother died before I was twenty. We had our little home and my brother and my three sisters and I lived on there. Three of us girls worked in the factories and one sister stayed at home and kept house for us. Our combined wages made a pretty good income. We lived well, dressed well, and were very happy. My brother married and went West to live. The housekeeping sister married next and then my youngest sister found a husband. That broke up the home, for the two that were left couldn't afford to keep it up. We took a couple of rooms and did our little housekeeping early in the morning before we went to work.

At this time there came a break in the monotony of my life. I married a young man I had known for a number of years. He was an iron molder and made good wages. We went to housekeeping and I thought my collar starching days were over forever. But my husband was taken ill, and before I realized that he was seriously sick I was a widow with a two-year-old daughter to support.

I naturally thought of the factory, but a friend who kept a grocery store begged me to come to live with her and help her with the business. I stayed at the store for eighteen months and at the end of that time I married again, a young telegraph operator I met in the store.

You see I have really done my best to fulfill what the ministers and others often tell us is the true destiny of a woman—to be a wife and mother. But the fates have been against me. My second husband had incipient consumption when I married him, altho neither of us knew it. He died after a short illness and six months later my little boy was born. Before the baby was a month old I was back in the factory, a starcher girl once more. Except for this interval of six years I have earned my living starching collars at four cents the dozen.

I have managed to bring up my two children fairly well. They have gone to school and my daughter has had music and dancing lessons. She is thirteen now and beginning to think of learning a trade. I shall not allow her to become a starcher. My boy is ten. He is very fond of his books and I shall try to put him through the high school. I don't know exactly how it is to be done, especially if the Employers' Association succeeds in cutting our wages in half.

There are many married women and widows in the factories in Troy. Of the married women, some have been deserted and others have gone to work because their husbands could not seem to make a living. It seems to me that in a community where the women greatly outnumber the men, the men get discouraged and deteriorate. Very few of the girls in Troy look forward with enthusiasm to marriage. If they are making fairly good wages they hesitate before giving up their jobs. They have too many object lessons around them of women who have come back to the factories after a few years of married life, all their gaiety and high spirits gone and two or three children at

An Anonymous Collar Starcher

home to support. It is a mystery to me how they bring up their children so well. I had friends to help me with mine and I suppose the others have. It means sitting up until all hours sewing, mending, and washing little clothes. After all, a working mother is like any other woman; she wants her children to wear pretty dresses and starched white petticoats.

Collar starching cannot be classed with unskilled labor. It requires considerable intelligence and a knack of handling the starch so as to get it smoothly through the goods. The starchers work very quickly, of course. They have to, both for the sake of the collars and for the sake of their wages. It is possible to starch fifty dozen or more a day, depending on the style of collar. I have often done so. If the work kept up at such a pace a starcher's wages would amount to ten or twelve dollars a week, but, unfortunately, the busy season lasts only three months in the year. A good starcher makes as high as fifteen or sixteen dollars a week during those three months. The rest of the year she is lucky if she makes seven dollars a week. The average, I think, is about six. The average wage the year round is between eight and nine dollars.

In order to make good money during the busy season I get up at half-past five in the morning, prepare a hasty breakfast, leaving the dishes for my daughter to wash. By half-past six I am at work. In the middle of the morning I stop just long enough to take a cup of coffee and a piece of bread, which stay me until lunchtime. Ten minutes' pause for lunch and I am hard at work again. Sometimes I work as late as eight o'clock. When I get home my daughter has my dinner ready for me. A year or two ago I used to have to get it myself after the work was over. Then, often there was washing to be done, for I am obliged in my factory to wear a white gown. Dark calico doesn't present such an attractive appearance, you know.

Many women have it harder than I. One friend of mine has two children and a bedridden mother to care for after hours, and just before the strike her husband was brought home with a broken hip.

I have said that a girl in our factory could make between eight and nine dollars a week the year round. The books will show that this is true, but the fact is you can't find out all there is to factory work by looking at the books. You can't find out, for instance, how much of the employees' wages go back to the firm in the shape of fines. To be docked two dollars a week is the commonest thing in the world at our factory. We expect it, in fact, and are thankful when it amounts to no more.

When I go to work in the morning I am given a slip of paper marked on one side "Received" and on the other "Returned." I mark on the one side the number of collars I receive. When the collars are starched I turn them over to boys from sixteen to twenty and they are sent to the drying rods. These boys mark on the other side of the slip the number of collars returned. If a boy makes a miscount or if for any reason at all the numbers do not tally on both sides of the slip, the starcher is docked. The amount docked from her wages is purely arbitrary. If she is short a dozen of work she is charged from fifty cents to a dollar. If the return side contains a dozen more collars than the starcher appears to have received the starcher is docked ten cents and is not paid for the work she is credited with doing. The great majority of the girls are docked every week in this matter of the received and returned slip. The boys are never docked, it being assumed, apparently, that they never make mistakes. But we no longer even wonder why these unjust distinctions are made.

If a starcher drops one collar on the floor she is docked five dozen collars. In other words for every collar dropped on the floor the girl must starch five dozen collars for nothing. The starcher is even held responsible after the collars leave her hands. If the bars on which the collars are dried happen to be dirty, the starcher is fined, although the bars are supposed to be cleaned by other workers. If a collar drops from the cleaning bars and is found on the floor, the four girls whose work is nearest are fined. Since it is not possible accurately to locate the careless one the four are punished in order to fine the right one.

These are not all the excuses for docking, but they are the most flagrant and unjust ones. It has been said on good authority that our firm alone has recovered from its employees, in fines, *$159,900*, during the past ten years.

Our position seemed pretty hopeless last August, just a year ago, when our present troubles began. At that time several firms in the association put in starching machines. We had no objection to machines, nor have we now, provided the machines do the work. We would welcome any device which made our task easier or enabled us to turn out more work. I want to make that point clear at the outset.

The machines were brought in but the table starchers were not put to work on them at once. Young girls were brought in from the outside and were set to work in a room by themselves. These girls until just before the strike were not subjected to the same conditions that the table starchers were under. They were given only the easiest work; they were allowed helpers, so that they never had to leave their tables. In this way they were able to make very fair wages, the payroll, in fact, showing they received about the same as the table starchers, who were receiving larger pay per dozen collars. Then the table starchers were informed that hereafter all starching would be done by machinery and that wages would be cut to two cents a dozen. At the same time they began to lay off ten girls a week.

The great majority of the girls were entirely ignorant of labor union methods. Most of us had never even read any labor literature. But every one of us realized that the time had come when we must organize. The first thing the union did was to agree, instead of having these girls laid off, to share our work with them. We were anxious to retain the girls for more reasons than one. For instance, we were puzzled to understand why they were laid off. We knew that there was no shortage of work, for the firms were actually sending work out to other shops.

We next agreed to try the machines, and we maintain that we did give them a fair trial. They were put in some time in August, and the strike did not come until the 4th of May following. We experimented with them long enough to convince all the starchers, including the new ones who had never starched after the tables, that the machines did not and could not starch the collars. The starchers were supposed to only have to rub the work over lightly after it left the machines, but the fact is they had to do as much to the collars after they came out of the machine as they did to the hand-starched work. The machine work resulted in stiff welts in the loose linings of the collars, and these welts we had to beat and soak out, and often restarch the whole collar, making the process longer and harder than it had ever been, with a cut of fifty percent in our wages.

Why should the firms have put in such machines? We asked ourselves the question, and at first it seemed like another of the experiments they try from time to time, experiments which the workers are made to pay for. One such experiment was the use of a certain kind of starch, presumably a cheaper quality than had been used, for the end and aim of all manufacturers is, of course, to lower the cost of production. I shall never forget that starch. It was a German importation. We tried very hard to use it, knowing, of course, that we would be docked if the work was unsatisfactory. It was impossible for us to get it into the linen, and our work all came out soft. We were docked, tried the starch again and were again docked. Then we struck, but our union was too weak to hold out. We went back, tried the starch three days more with the same result and finally convinced the firm that the starch was no good. We paid for that experiment with something like a week's wages.

Knowing the uselessness of combating an experiment we kept on at the machines for a little while after we saw that they could not do the work. The factory was all upside down. One day one thing would be said and the next day another. Three cents a dozen for hand work began to be talked about, and then, all of a sudden, the light broke upon us. The whole thing was clear. The machines were merely a subterfuge to reduce wages.

The table starchers and the machine starchers held a meeting and discussed the situation. We agreed that we could not stand a reduction of fifty percent. We felt that we should have to grant something to save ourselves, so we agreed to accept a reduction of twenty-five percent by working after the machines, with bunchers and hangers up, but we were firm in our determination to stand by our old wages for table work. Meanwhile small groups of girls were being discharged and laid off.

We appointed a committee to call on the head of the firm. He refused to let the committee into his office. Twice was the committee refused an interview. Then we struck. The girls remained in the workrooms until one of the firm came in. He said that he had business at the armory and could not talk to them. The leader asked when he would be willing to discuss matters. He said: "You must first go back to work, and I will consider about giving you a hearing at some future date."

The girls refused to go back to work until the matter of discharging and the matter of wages were discussed, and that night they were all discharged.

Several attempts were made to patch up the trouble. The Commissioner of Labor tried to intervene and the State Board of Mediation, I think it is called, did what it could. The Chamber of Commerce also tried. Arbitration was all the girls asked for, but they insisted that the arbi-

An Anonymous Collar Starcher

tration come before they went back to work. President Shea of the Federation of Labor and George Waldron, a delegate of the federation, were chosen to confer with our firm. The firm referred them to the Manufacturers' Association. The association refused to meet the men but agreed to meet a committee of the starchers. On May 11 the starchers met the association, and two days later they met them again. Nothing came of either meeting, and a few days later all the girls walked out, not only from our factory, but from the nine in the association. The immediate cause of the sympathetic strike was the action of the other factories in taking the laundry work of the factory where the strike occurred. We have been much blamed for this sympathetic strike. As for me, I cannot see the difference between our sympathetic strike and the sympathetic action of the factories in the association.

We have been out ever since. At first there were small riots. We picketed the factories and tried by all peaceable means to prevent the non-union girls hired to take our places from entering. Some of them turned back ashamed, but others persisted in going in. These girls had their hair pulled and their faces slapped. I am not concealing that. The non-union girls were certainly terrorized. A few of them were handled pretty roughly. We have been denounced for this. Well, there may be better methods of preventing thoughtless and heartless girls from injuring their class, and thereby injuring themselves. I wish I knew what they were. Many of these girls were not in the permanent working class. They became strikebreakers from ignorance and want of reflection, most of them. Others probably belonged to the class that out of pure snobbery opposes organization. They will not join a union because they do not wish to officially ally themselves with the working classes.

We have allied ourselves with the national body of the Laundry Workers' Union and receive strike benefits from them. Some of the girls whose sisters are working, voluntarily do without the benefit money; so there is enough to support the others. Some have left Troy and have found work in other towns. The rest of us are still doing picket duty and are holding the union together in all ways we know of. We have every confidence in our leaders.

The sympathy we have met with in the town has been very encouraging. One merchant gave us *$500* cash and another gives us *$25* a week. Of course most of the merchants are afraid to offend the manufacturers, whose patronage is worth more than that of the workers. The churches generally are thoroughly down on the strikers and our own ministers tell us that we ought to submit ourselves to the terms our kind employers are good enough to offer us. The head of my firm is one of the most generous contributors to the Y.M.C.A. and has helped build and renovate two churches. He is called an active Christian and is very much looked up to by the best people in Troy. Others in the Employers' Association are splendid churchmen. The Sunday schools and the church societies have a great hold on many of the stitchers and banders. For this reason large numbers of them hold out against a sympathetic strike of the operatives. They tell us privately that they hope we will win

An Anonymous Collar Starcher

and if we do they will probably form unions of their own. That is always the way and we do not complain.

Meanwhile there is one comforting feature: the Employers' Association, in order to save money, is spending it. They have to send all their laundry work out of town to get it done. Some of it goes as far away as Chicago. Their express bills must be something awful.

There is one more little bit of comfort. You ought to see how fat and rosy the girls are getting in the open air. Girls who didn't look like anything are as pretty as pinks since they began to do picket duty.

Elias Garza
Mexican American

❦

The people of Mexican ancestry who today call themselves La Raza, Chicano, or Mexican American were absorbed into the United States after a successful war of conquest in the 1840s brought most of the Southwest under American control. Though guaranteed their rights and lands by treaty, Chicanos soon found these promises empty. They were deprived of their best lands, denied the vote, and reduced to the status of peasants under white authority. By the beginning of the twentieth century Texas Rangers were directing an attack on Chicanos similar to Ku Klux Klan attacks on Blacks. A reporter for

Elias Garza, Mexican American

World's Week *wrote: "Some rangers have degenerated into common man-killers. There is no penalty for killing, for no jury would ever convict a white man for shooting a Mexican."*

The working Chicano had to battle salary differentials that paid him far less than whites for the same work. When union organization was attempted and strikes and violence flared in Arizona copper mines and elsewhere, state militia were summoned to suppress Chicano militancy. White judges, schoolteachers, and editors mounted a campaign that undermined Chicano economic and cultural independence throughout the Southwest.

Elias Garza, a native of Cuernavaca, found little to enjoy during his long stays in the United States. This is his story as recorded by a social worker fifty years ago.

My life is a real story, especially here in the United States where they drive one crazy from working so much. They squeeze one here until one is left useless, and then one has to go back to Mexico to be a burden to one's countrymen. But the trouble is that is true not only here but over there also. . . .

I began to work when I was twelve years old. My mother was a servant and I worked in one of those old mills which ground sugar cane. I took charge of driving the oxen. They called me the driver. This was on the estate of La Piedad, Michoacán. I think that they paid me $.25 a day and I had to go round and round the mill from the time the sun rose until it set. My mother, as well

§ *141* §

as I, had to work, because my father died when I was very small.

I went on in that way until when I was fifteen or sixteen I planted corn on my own account on shares. The owners gave us the seed, the animals, and the land, but it turned out that when the crop was harvested there wasn't anything left for us even if we had worked very hard. That was terrible. Those landowners were robbers.

At that time I heard that there were some good jobs here in the United States and that good money could be made. Some other friends accompanied me and we went first to Mexico City and from there we came to Ciudad Juárez. We then went to El Paso and there we took a *renganche* for Kansas. We worked on the tracks, taking up and laying down the rails, removing the old ties and putting in new, and doing all kinds of hard work. They only paid us $1.50 and exploited us without mercy in the commissary camp, for they sold us everything very high. Nevertheless as at that time things generally were cheap I managed to make a little money with which I went back to La Piedad to see my mother. She died a little later and this left me very sad.

I decided to come back to the United States, and I came to Los Angeles, California. Here I married a Mexican young lady. I went to work in a stone quarry. I placed the dynamite and did other work which took some care. They paid me $1.95 a day but I worked ten hours. Later I worked at a railroad station. I worked as a riveter, working a pressure gun for riveting. At that work I earned $1.50 a day for nine hours, but it was very hard. My wife died at that time.

Elias Garza, Mexican American

I then got work in a packing plant. I began by earning $1.25 a day there for nine hours of work and I got to earn $4.00 a day for eight hours work. I learned to skin hogs there and slaughter them also. The work was very hard. Later I was married to a woman from San Antonio, Texas. She was young, beautiful, white, and she had two little children who became my stepchildren. We went to Mexico together. We boarded ship at San Pedro and from there went to Mazatlán until we got to Michoacán. We saw that things were bad there, for that was in *1912*, and the disorders of the revolution had already started; so we came back to the United States by way of Laredo, Texas.

In San Antonio we were under contract to go and pick cotton in a camp in the valley of the Rio Grande. A group of countrymen and my wife and I went to pick. When we arrived at the camp the planter gave us an old hovel which had been used as a chicken house before, to live in, out in the open. I didn't want to live there and told him that if he didn't give us a little house which was a little better we would go. He told us to go, and my wife and I and my children were leaving when the sheriff fell upon us. He took me to the jail and there the planter told them that I wanted to leave without paying him for my passage. He charged me twice the cost of the transportation, and though I tried first not to pay him, and then to pay him what it cost, I couldn't do anything. The authorities would only pay attention to him, and as they were in league with him they told me that if I didn't pay they would take my wife and my little children to work. Then I paid them. From there we went to Dallas, Texas, from where we worked on the tracks as far as El Paso. I kept on at the same work towards Tucson, Arizona, until I got to Los Angeles. I have worked in the packing plants here since then, in cement and other jobs, even as a farm laborer. In spite of it all I have managed to save some money with which I have bought this automobile and some clothes. I have now decided to work in the colony in Mexico and not come back to this country where I have left the best of my youth.

I learned a little English here from hearing it so much. I can read and write it, but I don't even like to deal with those *bolillos* for the truth is that they don't like the Mexicans. Even the *pochos* don't like us. I have scarcely been able to stand up for my rights with the little English that I have learned, but I would like to know a lot of English so as to tell them what they are and in order to defend my poor countrymen. . . .

Once a poor Mexican bought a bottle of whiskey to take to his house to drink it. He had put it in the back pocket of his trousers. That was at night and he was going home. He stopped in front of a workshop to see some goods when he noticed that a policeman was drawing near. Then he slyly put his hand to his back pocket in order to take the little bottle out and perhaps throw it away when the policeman, without more ado, fired a shot at him and killed him. They didn't do anything to that policeman; he is going about free. And there have been an infinite number of cases like that.

I know of others who at work in the factories have lost an arm or a leg, and they haven't been given a thing. What they do is to take away their jobs. That is why we don't like these people.

Elias Garza, Mexican American

I almost am, and almost am not, a Catholic. I remember that when I was very little, over there in Cuernavaca, my mother took me to some exercises of Holy Week and that the priest told all those who were in the church that they should cry for their sins before Christ there in the temple, and they all began to weep and to cry out all that they had done, even my own mother. But I couldn't weep nor did I want to cry out my sins. Since that time I have almost not gone back to the church nor do I pray at home.

I read few newspapers for they almost don't say anything but lies and one comes out from work so tired that one doesn't even want to read papers of any kind. I have almost never read books; once in a long time I do read books of stories of Mexicans.

I have always tried to be close to my countrymen and defend them, but there are some who are neither united nor do they want to defend themselves; that is why the Americans look down on us as they do.

An Anonymous Policeman

By the end of the nineteenth century, many moralists, ministers, and reformers had denounced American cities as ungovernable dens of vice, corruption, and lawlessness. Charged with keeping this bubbling caldron from boiling over was the lowly cop on the beat. He was asked to bring public behavior into line with society's professed moral standards, armed with a billy club, a pistol, and an inadequate knowledge and appreciation of civil liberties and justice. He was hamstrung by a top command who took orders from the political and business forces that benefited from crime. Police missions aimed at crime-

An Anonymous Policeman

land's powerful leaders were very rare.

Police departments did not select recruits with any regard for moral qualities. In fact, recruits were usually obliged to use bribes and politics to join the force. Since police work was dangerous and not particularly well paid, police generally came from the lower classes and were overawed by those with power or money.

In 1895, Police Captain Max F. Schmittberger testified before a state commission that New York City's entire Police Department was "rotten to the core." It took $600 to make an officer a sergeant, $14,000 to make him a captain. "It's either politics or money," he stated, "that moves a man to higher command." Describing the collapse of the justice system in the nation's largest city, he used this phrase: "The pillars of the church are falling and have fallen."

Three years after Captain Schmittberger's testimony, another citizen, fulfilling a boyhood dream, joined the New York Police Department. This is his story.

When I got to be twenty-one years of age I tried to get on the police force, and a politician told me that he would put me on for $300. I had been working as a clerk for a junkman in Pearl Street and had saved a little money and I agreed to pay $300. I gave it to the politician in the back room of a saloon on William Street, and he counted the money and said that he would see me through. He told the proprietor of the place to enclose the money in an envelope, and put it in his safe, which was done.

I made my application and waited three months, but was turned down.

The politician told me that I would have to raise $300 more, and so I went back to clerking till the beginning of 1898 when I was ready for another attempt to get on the force. I made application to the Civil Service Commissioners and received a copy of the requirements, which seemed to show that I was not eligible.

Two policemen told me that the civil service people were square, and that money had nothing to do with passing examinations. I found that there was a fight on under the surface between the civil service schools and the politicians because the schools were putting men on the force who had paid nothing to their leaders.

I told my district leader that I was going to the school and he swore at me.

Six months after I had entered the school I was examined by the Civil Service Commissioners and passed with 81 percent physical and 83 percent mental, and a month later I was appointed by the police commissioner. That was in November, 1898.

I was assigned to duty in the precinct where I lived, and reported to the captain, who put me on probation for 30 days. Each week day I attended the police school of instruction, where I kept up athletics and learned drill and rules, and each night I went out with a policeman, who "broke me in" to the duties, and whom I assisted in making arrests.

The politician met me on the street, shook his fist in my face, and swore that he would have me dismissed from the force if I didn't "put up." I told him he was a "has been," and that no one had to "put up" now. He made trouble for me two or three times after that by means of a sergeant who worked one night and day and a roundsman who was always reporting me. Finally I got myself transferred out of his district, when I thought I was safe, but he kept after me by means of another leader, till at last I gave him $200 to "call it square."

The influence of the politicians over the police force has been growing weaker all the time, and some of the sergeants and captains now refuse to take orders from the district leaders.

The politicians' "pull" is founded on the fact that they make the mayor who makes the police commissioner. So when they elect a mayor they ask for a commissioner who will suit them, and when he is in office they can make it very hot for a captain who tries to enforce blue laws. They can move the captains around, putting one who does as he is told in a place where he can make $30,000 a year in addition to salary, and another in a place where he cannot make a cent extra.

So if a policeman disturbs "good people who are paying tribute" the district leader complains to the captain of the precinct, and if he does not mend matters a complaint of the captain is made to the commissioner. But this seldom happens. The patrolman who insisted on enforcing all the laws would be an idiot. He would not last a month, and would be thrown out a broken and disgraced man. His officers and comrades would see to that.

How far this business of protecting people who violate laws goes I don't know. It used to include pickpockets, tin-horn gamblers with brace games, bunco men, green goods and knock-out-drops operators, and burglars—pretty nearly all sorts of regular operators. It isn't anything like as complete now as it used to be. Still there are pickpockets now operating about the Bridge, and how could they do it unless the police were fixed?

Some are let work and some are taken in, and there must be a reason for the difference of treatment. Pickpockets, like detectives, work in couples, and I've known one to come up to a pair of plainclothes men, and say:

"The other fellow has *$150.*"

One of the detectives collars the other pickpocket, and says: "I guess I'll have to take you up to the station house and 'mug' you (take photograph for Rogue's Gallery)."

"Can't we fix it up?" says the pickpocket. "I have *$75.*"

"All right," says the detective, and takes the *$75* and the pickpocket trots on. Soon hears footsteps behind him, and another detective catches him. "Hey! What are you doing here? I'll have to take you in," says the second detective, and the pickpocket is collared again, and has to give up the other *$75* to get off. He goes away kicking himself.

Now, what did the first pickpocket get for betraying his partner? He must get something, for thieves have to live, and it costs money to support their families. The city isn't paying their salaries. It seems to stand to reason that the detectives must pay them by allowing them to work, and I suppose [it is the same] with the other criminals as with the pickpockets. But I don't pretend to know, and I'm sure that no one man knows all ends of this business of "protection," there's so much secrecy even between those most deeply engaged in it.

Since the last election we have had in office commissioners who could not be used by politicians to punish a man for doing his duty, and that's all right so far as it goes. But the men and their officers know perfectly well that the politicians are only down for the moment, and that they are coming back to power, so why should policemen make trouble for themselves by opposition to the present system.

That's the way we patrolmen look at the matter, so we go with the tide, taking what comes and not seeing any more than is good for us to see.

As I went around with the experienced policeman during my probation he taught me all the ropes, and explained that the greatest danger for a young man was from the temptation to arrest people who were "putting up."

"If you do that," he said, "the sergeant will work you forty-eight hours at a stretch, and finally break you."

It didn't take me long to find out that the sergeant could keep me on the go till I dropped if it suited him. That was when I went on regular duty at the end of a month. I arrested a saloonkeeper who forgot me, but who had put up for the wardman and the inspector's man. I got a hint to leave the man alone after that, but I wanted to make him understand that I had something to say as well as the big fellows. I took him in again for violating the Sunday law. He was discharged. Soon after that I came off duty and went on reserve. I went upstairs to the dormitory to sleep, having been on patrol for sixteen hours. I had not been in bed ten minutes when the sergeant called me down to the desk, and sent me out to see about some boys annoying householders ten blocks away. It was a fake report. When I came back he sent me out to a fire, and after that he found another special call to keep me busy till I had to go on patrol again. There are plenty of these special calls at a busy station house, and the sergeant can always make some if he wants them. I squared matters by apologizing to the saloonkeeper.

Before I got on the force I had heard that policemen made a deal of money in addition to their salaries, and after I got fairly to work I found that I was in it.

Of course, when promotions are paid for, the money has to come from "put ups." In Manhattan as much as $10,000 has sometimes been paid for a captaincy, but that is nothing if a man gets the right kind of a precinct where he can make from $20,000 to $50,000 a year. As I get them the rates for protection in Manhattan have been as follows per month:

Pool rooms, from $300 to $500; saloons, from $10 to $40; gambling houses, from $100 to $2,000; disorderly houses, $20 to $100; push carts, $2 per week each.

There's plenty of other "graft" that I don't know about; for instance, the detectives down in Wall Street make a lot of money somehow.

The push cart peddlers' money is collected by one of themselves. He goes among the carts and marks the stand of the man who has paid with white chalk, and the stand of the man who has not paid with blue chalk. The ignorant peddler does not notice.

Along comes the policeman on post and looks at the

carts. When he sees a blue mark on a cart he with his club poles the back off the peddler that owns it, moving him on while he lets his comrades stand.

In some of the precincts where there is plenty of "graft," the man who is violating the law pays the patrolman for closing his eyes, the captain for not breaking the patrolman, and the inspector for not breaking the captain. These are separate amounts. Say the patrolman gets $5 a month, the captain and inspector would get $20 each.

The most I ever made on any post was $156 a month. That was downtown in Manhattan on a beat that was about a mile and a half long. Every saloonkeeper on my post used to put up $5 a month for me and my partner in addition to the money given to the captain's agent—the inspector had no one collecting. There were twenty-five of these saloons and five gambling places, three of which gave me $10 a month, while two paid $5. From the women I and my partner, who patrolled the beat when I was off, got a total of about $75 a month. Of course, there were many who tried to do business without paying, but they soon found themselves in a hole because we enforced the law against them. Some patrolmen have made as high as $250 a month.

Besides the presents of money which naturally make policemen feel kindly disposed toward the givers there is free liquor. It is everywhere offered to the policemen, and it trips a good many of them up.

After a man has been on the force a little while he knows all the people who are "putting up," and grows to be very friendly with them. There are twenty places on my beat where I can tap at a side door and get a drink, and there are nearly as many where I can go in a back room and sleep while some one watches to give me warning if the roundsman comes in sight. So the temptation to take it easy and have a good time is very great, and on bad nights the policeman need not patrol his post unless he wants to.

New York policemen are just as honest as any other set of men, and this system of bribery is not their fault. It is the fault of the fool laws made for the benefit of old women who don't understand human nature. The laws pretend to try to abolish gambling and disorderly houses and to close drinking places on the only weekly holiday. That is all hypocrisy. Men always will gamble and drink. In the great cities of Europe there is a license system. If that were in force here it would put a stop to police bribery.

Mariner J. Kent
The Making of a Tramp

The one hundred novels of Horatio Alger in which ordinary people moved from rags to riches led many to think that such success was neither unusual nor hard to attain. It was easy to believe, despite the number of devastating economic depressions, that the unemployed or unemployable had no one but themselves to blame. The truth was that tramps, bums, and unemployables, including many disabled by industrial accidents and inhuman conditions, far outnumbered bankers, manufacturers, and merchants.

Vagabonds roamed the countryside, small towns, and

large cities looking for work, a hand out, a fresh start. Viewed as a dangerous if not unlawful element, they were often hounded by police and vigilantes and denounced by clergymen and upright citizens. And indeed, many ended up on police blotters for minor crimes.

While some were inveterate wanderers, unwilling to shoulder responsibility, others were working- or middle-class people who had been unlucky enough to fall from secure positions because of an economic or personal crisis, victims of a new industrial order that had no room for failures and not enough work for everyone. Very few climbed out of the abyss as easily as Mariner J. Kent, or looked forward as serenely to better days. Though his story's beginning is probably typical for many, its end makes him one of a lucky few.

After failing in a business venture I would not let go until the bitter end. I exhausted every avenue and byway of credit, borrowed from every living soul I knew, and pawned everything I possessed, save the clothes on my back. In the end when I shut up shop my assets were the frayed and seedy suit I wore and a dollar and a quarter in loose change. I was fifty years old, which was against me, and I had no particular calling to which I could turn my hand. But I had health and strength and the spirit of hustle in me.

I began my fight for life the first week in September last. First I booked myself at a fifteen-cent lodging house on the Bowery, and invested a quarter in meal tickets at a restaurant, which offers the following bill of fare: Pint of coffee and bread, *1* cent; pint of soup and bread, *1* cent; beef stew and bread, *2* cents; baked beans and bread, *2* cents; bread pudding, *2* cents.

Then began the hunt for work. Up early in the morning to scan the advertising columns of the morning dailies and then an all day tramp in search of a job, an asking in my case that always met with a refusal. In my experience I found that for every situation there were from ten to fifty applicants, and that the possibility of securing employment by answering advertisements was as remote as the finding of a needle in a hay mow. As has before been written, many came but few were chosen.

At the end of five days I was penniless. I had lived too high. Ten cents a day for food and fifteen cents a night for lodging might do for a high-roller, but not for a poor man looking for work. So I hunted the parks and joined the ranks of the homeless men who "carry the stick." This term is an elastic one, and means sleeping on a bench in a park or in a furniture van or in a beer dive, as the case may be, or wandering to and fro until the night is spent. The regular panhandlers and hoboes I avoided, and my chance companions of the parks as a class were men who would work if they could get it to do, a class of poor and friendless men that become numerous in a great city; such a class of men as a city magistrate recently said ought to commit suicide because of their uselessness. Really they are no worse than most successful men who, in their egotism, are prone to think that poverty is a crime. Yet to the taunts of the successful and opulent these men, with hollow eyes and shrunken bellies, might say:

> *We are the slaves, the needy knaves*
>   *Ye spit upon with scorn—*
> *The spawn of earth, of nameless birth,*
>   *And basely bred as born;*
> *Yet know, ye soft and silken fools,*
>   *Were we the thing you say,*
> *Your broad domains, your coffered gains,*
>   *Your lives were ours today.*

At the very first of my consorting with the "bench-warmers" I noticed the lack of fellowship among them, the absence of that free masonry which exists among seasoned tramps to a high degree. Panhandlers and hoboes are socially inclined when congregated, and jovial when by hook or crook they have got under their jackets a modicum of stale beer or bootleg whiskey. They chat and lay plans for foraging and for deeds of petty larceny, or discuss with animation the latest dodge in alms-asking. But the array of forlorn men who camp in the public parks are an inert mass of worn and wretched humanity. They huddle together perforce on the narrow benches, but they seldom speak to each other, and then in low and spiritless tones. They are strangers in an inhospitable land, and in their misery they shrink from contact with unkind man, even tho he be one of their own ilk. Certainly one as low as they have become cannot succor them or cheer their drooping spirits. Sodden and hopeless, they doze under the trees that bar the rays of the electric lights, living shadows of silent despair.

During all the weeks I was among these unhappy men there was never a wrangle or approach to a quarrel. They had no inclination or heart to dispute; and on the other hand a peal of laughter, God help them, was a thing of the past. A snatch of a cheering song or an enlivening story from any one of that desolate throng would have been as strange and unnatural as a circus in a graveyard. It is doubtful if serious thought had longer a place in their benumbed brains, but the fiends of retrospection and introspection were there to wring their hearts while hunger gnawed at their vitals.

One of the saddest things about the men of the parks is their condition as compared to age. They are not as a class old and worn-out men, for the proportion of men under fifty is greater than that of men above that age, while the boys from sixteen to twenty outnumber the men of fifty and past. The preponderance of men from twenty-five to forty years of age is a striking commentary upon a social condition that denies a man the privilege to labor that he may live.

These men work at intervals at some menial employment. They find an odd job now and then, but their seedy appearance precludes the obtaining of a desirable or permanent position, except in rare cases. With the little money thus earned they enjoy the luxury of a cheap bed, the keen satisfaction of a ten-cent meal, the joy of a good wash, the wholesomeness of a clean shirt and the comfort of whole socks. Their good fortune is usually short-lived, lasting only a day and a night perhaps, and then they take to the benches in the parks again. And so their jaded lives go to the end, and the end is reached in various ways. Many of the boys and younger men and some of the older men drift into crime and find a place in the workhouse or penitentiary; criminals not from inclination, but because of their cruel environment. The end of others is the hospital and the potter's field. Some drift into the country and in most cases better their condition. The army and navy weed the ranks of the physically best. A few find employment and take their places among men again. The remainder degenerate into full-fledged tramps, and enter the domain of besotted manhood by the hideous gate that opens inward, but never outward. The places of those who pass out by these devious ways are quickly filled by the new recruits who have enlisted under the black flag of hunger.

During the first week of my enforced sojourn in the parks my mental and physical sufferings were greater than in subsequent weeks. My mind was in a complex state. I was not hopeless, nor did I become so at any stage of the game. I keenly felt the humiliation of my position, and the sense of disbarment from all sweetness of life was overwhelming. I dreaded to meet anyone that I knew, lest he should apprehend my outcast state. Physically I was demoralized. From want of regular sleep my brain became wearied and sluggish. The pangs of hunger tormented me and sapped my energy. As yet I had not eaten of the bread of charity, but at the end of the week of starvation the boast of a lifetime that I would steal before I would beg seemed trivial. At midnight on Sunday I fell into the long line of men waiting for the portion of stale bread that a philanthropic baker nightly doles out to the homeless. The line is always formed ahead of time, for the first two that arrive are given a double portion, for which they sweep the sidewalk of crumbs, while those at the end of the line go away empty handed when it happens that the supply of bread is short. While I awaited my turn my thoughts were busy. On one side of the array of hungry men loomed the great building erected by a merchant prince, who added to his tens of millions by driving small dealers out of business and by cutting the wages of labor. On the other side rose the marble walls of Grace Church, the worshiping place of the rich and powerful. The tall and ornate spire pointing heavenward recalled the words of the Galilean: "He that cometh to me shall never hunger; and he that believeth on me shall never thirst." But on that Sunday night of which I write the hungry were fed by the baker and not by the church. As the men received their allotted portion they slunk away, not in groups or pairs, but solitary and alone, munching the bread as they went. The status of the men of the parks was easily determined by the way they ate their bread. The newcomers ate ravenously; those of longer experience more slowly but with evident relish, while the old timers ate with an effort, forcing the bread down as a necessity to life. A continuous diet of bread alone does not satisfy the inner man, and in this connection one of the bread eaters unintentionally said a good thing. He voiced the cry of his stomach and described his emaciated condition by the single remark that the skin was cracking on his bones for the lack of meat. As for myself, I ate the bread of charity for the first time in my life, and it did not choke me; on the contrary, it appeased my fierce hunger. Swelling it up with water from the fountain at the park, I settled into a seat on a bench and slept until an officer on his morning round aroused me with a rough shake and the command to "Wake up and take a walk."

The second week of struggle with poverty had its illuminations. I discovered two other bakers who gave out stale bread to the hungry; one at one o'clock and one at four o'clock in the morning. With the thrift inherited from my pilgrim ancestors, whose heroism on a continued diet of parched corn and lobster adorns the pages of history, I took in each night all three of the benevolent bakers and by this means had a supply of bread for the day, which I packed around until eaten. I also essayed to sell soap for a fake outfit that lives upon the credulity of the people in the tenement districts. At the end of three days, and I had striven to succeed, my commissions amounted to forty cents, and the boss of the wagon took away my basket, with the remark that I was far from being a crack-a-jack. With the money I arrayed myself in clean linen, had ten hours of sound sleep in bed, and soup at night and coffee in the morning at the penny restaurant, and a three-cent shave in the dago quarter.

My third week in the parks was uneventful.

The fourth week of my stay in the parks had its bright sides. Wandering about one morning after receiving my second installment of bread I reached the open market on the West Side. The fruit and produce dealers were opening up and the laden vans from the country were ranged in order in the square. Flitting about in the semidarkness were three shadowy forms. They sped through the streets adjoining the market in a noiseless fashion, stooping and rising at times as birds of prey swoop down and up. They were old and wizened women, bare of head and limb, who alertly gathered up the decaying fruit and vegetables that the dealers threw out. I joined the women in the quest and filled my pockets with pickings. They did not resent the encroachment upon their domain, and undisturbed I feasted upon the luscious finds. And thus each morning thereafter I had my fruit before breakfast. At the last of the week I received a job of delivering circulars at seventy-five cents a day, and this was permanent for one day in each week. The money thus earned allowed of two nights' rest in the lodging house, clean linen, and coffee each morning.

During the last weeks of my dire poverty but five nights of the seven were given to the parks. Two were spent in the lodging house, an enjoyment the proceeds of my one day's work permitted. My personal appearance, however, was most disreputable. My hair was untrimmed, my eyes sunken and dull, my neck scrawny, while my flaccid face had the putty hue of the half-fed and half-housed. The cheap straw hat I wore was stained with dust and humped by rain and midnight damp. My coat was faded and bulged and hung limply on my attenuated form. My ill-fitting vest flapped against my lean and shrunken abdomen. My trousers were a mass of triangular wrinkles, and the heels of my broken shoes were so run down on the outer side that I toed-in when walking.

My mental decadence had kept pace with the deterioration of my apparel. The trend of my thought was individualistic and scornful of the altruistic cant of a society based and sustained upon the profoundest egoism. I rejoiced that I was now no longer bound by conventions. With a cruel hand society had cast me out and a free outcast I would remain, indifferent to its frown or favor. The physical discomforts of an untrammeled life under the trees in the parks, or elsewhere, were trivial as compared to the obligations and limitations of social life. In me surged the spirit of Bobbie Burns's tinker, who sang:

> *A fig for those by law protected,*
> *Liberty's a glorious feast;*
> *Courts for cowards were erected,*
> *Churches built to please the priest.*

Thus I stood in the outer circle of the brotherhood of tramps. I had followed the process of tramp-making a long way; why not to the end? I had but a few years to live at the best; why not let them quietly slip away without toil or struggle? If on the easy tide of aimless living my oarless and rudderless bark drifted to oblivion, the sooner the better, for the end would bring rest. No face beckoned me back to earnest life, no voice called me to high and strenuous endeavor. So I joined the boundless concourse of lost men drifting on to what no one knows, to where no one cares.

But I was plucked as a brand from the burning by the sheer force of circumstances. The brisk fall trade called for an unusual number of circular distributors, and work was thrown in my way until I soon had constant employment at a dollar a day. I confined my weekly expenses to one dollar for lodgings, one dollar for food and fifty cents for laundry and incidentals, and in a comparatively short time I was presentably attired and mingling with my old acquaintances. Fortunately I secured a fairly lucrative position in time, and at this writing my prospects are of the brightest. But I do not scorn the homeless men whose lot I shared. A great wave of compassion fills my heart when I think of them, and I avoid the parks by night that the sight of their misery may not remain in my memory. No sadder picture can be drawn than that of these men of the parks cowering before the deadly face of want.

Recommended Reading

Ginger, Ray. *The Age of Excess, The United States from 1877 to 1914*. New York: Macmillan, 1965.

Hoogenboom, Ari and Hoogenboom, Olive, eds. *The Gilded Age*. Englewood Cliffs, N.J.: Prentice-Hall, 1967.

Jensen, Oliver, ed. *The Nineties*. New York: American Heritage, 1967.

Stein, Leon. *The Triangle Fire*. Philadelphia: J.B. Lippincott Co., 1962.

Sullivan, Mark. *Our Times: The United States 1900–1925*. 4 vols. New York: Charles Scribner's Sons, 1926.

Swados, Harvey, ed. *Years of Conscience, The Muckrakers*. Cleveland: World Publishing Co., 1962.

Bibliographical Note

This volume grew out of research into American minorities undertaken over the last dozen years. Its contents come from three major sources. The black cowpuncher's story is taken from *The Life and Adventures of Nat Love, Better Known in the Cattle Country as "Deadwood Dick," by Himself*, published in *1907* by Nat Love. Elias Garza's tale, taken from an interview in *1926* or *1927* by the Social Research Council, appeared in Manuel Gamio, ed., *The Mexican Immigrant: His Life Story*, published in *1931* by the University of Chicago. Both the Love volume and the Gamio book have been recently reprinted by Arno Press of New York City.

The other reminiscences came to our attention from a book

Bibliographical Note

picked up years ago in a secondhand bookstore: *The Life Stories of Undistinguished Americans, As Told by Themselves,* edited by Hamilton Holt in *1906.* A crusading journalist and founding member of the NAACP, Holt selected sixteen stories from the pages of *The Independent,* a liberal newsweekly he edited. Going back through the pages of *The Independent* we relived a part of the American past infrequently alluded to in history books. Holt had shifted his editorial focus to the lowly because he became convinced that common folk were swiftly coming into their own, and preservation of their historical record had valid sociological and literary justification. Together with Edwin E. Slosson, literary editor for *The Independent,* Holt printed six dozen autobiographies of ordinary people from 1902 to 1906. Not only did Slosson vouch for the accuracy of the memoirs, but he said the series was necessary for "the spirit of democracy, the discovery of the importance of the average man," for "it is the undistinguished people who move the world, or who prevent it from moving." Our selections from *The Independent* are offered in this belief.

The following photographs appear courtesy of the Museum of the City of New York:
Garment workers labor in a crowded sweatshop
At home under the dump on New York's Rivington Street
Members of New York's 20th Precinct police force
The feast of St. Rocco on New York's Mulberry Street
An Italian immigrant boy learns to write

Other photographs appear courtesy of the William Loren Katz collection.

WILLIAM LOREN KATZ

is the author of more than a dozen volumes on American minorities, including *Eyewitness: The Negro in American History*, and the six-volume *Minorities in American History* series.

Mr. Katz taught American history in secondary school for fifteen years and has written for *Saturday Review, Freedomways, Journal of Negro History,* and *Readers Digest*. A former scholar-in-residence at Columbia University, he has also taught Black history at New York University's Center for Afro-American Affairs.

He and his wife Jacqueline divide their time between England and New York City.

JACQUELINE HUNT KATZ

was born in Portsmouth, England, and attended English schools. In *1964* she joined the staff of the International Commission of Jurists in Geneva, Switzerland, a non-governmental agency devoted to exposing violations of human rights throughout the world. After work-associated travel in Asian, African, and European nations, she was assigned to the New York office of ICJ, where she met and began working with William Loren Katz on the research for his books.

CARNEGIE PUBLIC LIBRARY
ROBINSON, ILLINOIS